EDMUND SPENSER
AND THE
FAERIE QUEENE

EDMUND SPENSER

AND THE

FAERIE QUEENE

By

LEICESTER BRADNER

THE UNIVERSITY OF CHICAGO PRESS

CHICAGO & LONDON

The publication of this volume has been aided by a grant from the American Council of Learned Societies from a fund provided by the Carnegie Corporation of New York.

International Standard Book Number: 0-226-07051-4

THE UNIVERSITY OF CHICAGO PRESS, CHICAGO 60637

The University of Chicago Press, Ltd., London

c

6001017797X

To

H. P. B.

"Most happy letters fram'd by skilfull trade"

PREFACE

THIS is not a book for Spenser scholars. It is an attempt to arouse in the educated general reader a desire to become acquainted with one of the great classics of English literature which is at present suffering from unmerited neglect. For this reason the treatment has been to present the *Faerie Queene* as it will appear to a person who has no professional interest in it. As far as possible all questions of sources, influences, and purely contemporary allegorical allusions have been omitted. Knowledge of such matters adds considerably to the understanding of the poem on the part of an advanced student of literary history; it is of little value to a reader approaching Spenser for the first time.

As a further step in carrying out this aim I have somewhat modernized the text of the poems in a number of places in my quotations. I have not tried to modernize the spelling in general. Because of Spenser's intentionally archaic style, any attempt to produce a completely modern text would create more problems than it would solve. The rhyme words alone would form an almost insuperable obstacle; and many truncated forms, such as "gan" for "began," would be intolerable in a text otherwise modernized, yet the meter will not allow of their expansion. I have changed only two old words into modern metrical equivalents of the same meaning. Spenser scholars may amuse themselves by hunting for them. Capitalization has been reduced to current practice, and the punctuation has been similarly changed wherever it was likely to cause difficulty.

If the intelligent modern reader neglects Spenser, he cannot be much blamed for his attitude. He is only putting a reasonable interpretation on what he has read about Spenser in the editorial material in his Freshman anthology of literature or in most of the standard lives of the poet before Professor Judson's recent biography. From editors of anthologies he learns that Spenser's story is uninteresting, that the meaning of his allegory is unimportant, that he should be read only for the beauty of his verse. When, after this, he is hypocritically told that Spenser is one of our greatest writers, he naturally concludes that there is some mistake and that if Spenser really was the poets' poet it just shows how little sense poets have. In the biographical sketches he finds Spenser portrayed as a rather visionary creature, unsuccessful in coping with politicians at court or rebels in Ireland, who retired in his mind to a dream world of fairyland in which medieval knights and Platonic philosophy seem to be mixed up in some strange way.

Naturally the scholars who specialize in Spenser have long ago discarded these nineteenth-century misconceptions. To them the poet is known as a man of keen intelligence and practical ability. They know that his superb literary craftsmanship was not wasted upon idle dreams. That their view is not shared by readers of the college-graduate group is partly the fault of scholars in writing for each other instead of for the public and partly the fault of modern sophisticates to whom beauty such as Spenser creates is somehow suspect. For such readers it is necessary to demonstrate through a fresh examination of his life and of the *Faerie Queene* that he has something to offer.

Preface

They must be led to respect his character and to find it interesting by modern standards, and they must be shown that the *Faerie Queene* is not a museum piece but a living criticism of life. To this task the present work is dedicated.

It is obvious that in a work of this sort I am deeply indebted to the whole company of Spenser students and more especially to a few of the classics in this field. Edwin Greenlaw's *Spenser's Historical Allegory* and W. L. Renwick's *Edmund Spenser: An Essay on Renaissance Poetry* have long been indispensable to an understanding of the *Faerie Queene*, and C. S. Lewis' chapter on Spenser in his *Allegory of Love* is of the utmost importance. To these I would add Mrs. Josephine W. Bennett's recent book, *The Evolution of the Faerie Queene*. Alexander C. Judson's *Life of Edmund Spenser*, an inestimable boon to all workers in the Elizabethan field, unfortunately did not appear until I had completed my own account. I have omitted specific statements of the details of my debt to these and other scholars. To my colleagues they will be evident; to others they are irrelevant.

Finally, it is a pleasure to thank those who read portions of this book before publication: Rosemond Tuve, Josephine W. Bennett, Theodore H. Banks, Douglas Bush, Don C. Allen, S. Foster Damon, C. Arthur Lynch, and Israel J. Kapstein. Without their comments and encouragement my task would have been much longer and lonelier.

LEICESTER BRADNER

BROWN UNIVERSITY

TABLE OF CONTENTS

[xi]

CHAPTER I

INTRODUCTION

THE sixteenth century was an age of violence, change, and confusion. Old ways of life were broken up; conventional views were attacked; mental and physical horizons were expanded. The century began with the revolt of Luther against the papacy on moral and religious grounds, which was followed by the revolt of Henry VIII on political grounds; and neither was so far-reaching or dangerous as the revolt of Calvin in the middle of the century, which set up the basic rationale of all nonconformity to an established church. In the field of politics the treatises of Erasmus and others on the Christian training of princes made little headway against the codification by Machiavelli of the ways, moral or immoral, by which a prince really succeeds in attaining absolute power. Christian monarchs plotted one another's destruction and called in the aid of the Turk if their own resources were insufficient. Revolts flared in France and the Netherlands; the queen of Scotland was imprisoned by her own subjects and executed later by the English.

The map of the world and the cosmology of the universe were no less drastically altered. The Americas were discovered just as the century came in, and the conquests of Cortez and Pizzaro were the epics of discovery on land, as were the voyages of Magellan and Drake at sea. While Copernicus' substitution of the sun for the earth as the center of the known universe took two generations to be accepted widely, it nevertheless cast grave doubts in many minds as to the validity of the Ptolemaic system which had reigned supreme for more than a thousand years.

England came in for its full share of the vicissitudes of the century. The wealth of Henry VII and the ambition of Henry VIII made it a great power in the first half of the century, but the religious upheavals and ruinous financial policies of the short reigns of Edward and Mary reduced it to impotence. Indeed, for a time it was a mere satellite of Spain. When Elizabeth came to the throne in 1559 and set out to reform both finance and religion, it was the fourth time in thirty years that the national church changed its complexion. No wonder that many people simply conformed in the belief that this latest change would not last. Elizabeth's foreign policy was the despair of her councilors, and her constant shifting and changing alternately displeased either her Catholic or her Protestant subjects— but it worked. By playing off one enemy against another for a whole generation she built up her treasury, the strength of her navy, and the morale of her people to the point where a successful war against Spain was possible. It was this war, begun in the Netherlands in 1585 and fought in two oceans for some fifteen years, which showed the English that they were now an even greater power than under Henry VIII and stirred them to produce one of the world's greatest outbursts of literature in the closing years of Elizabeth's reign.

Among the great writers of this period none is so truly and characteristically Elizabethan as Edmund Spenser. Like Shakespeare he rose from a humble background to a position of wealth and fame, showing an extraordinary ability to deal with the world on its own terms. Unlike Shakespeare he moved habitually among men of power and men of action. The earl of Leicester and his nephew

Introduction

Sir Philip Sidney; Lord Grey, who was one of the leading military men in England; Sir Walter Raleigh, soldier, discoverer, and planter of colonies; John and Thomas Norris, presidents of Munster in Ireland—these were the men whom Spenser knew and on whom he based the heroes of his great poem. His life reads like a youngster's dream come true. Entering Cambridge, the cradle of Puritanism, as a charity student, he did so well in his studies that he won a position as secretary to an important bishop, John Young. Leaving Young after a year, he went to Leicester House, where he ran errands and took dictation for the great earl and had a taste of court life. Before he had time to get tired of this, he obtained the exciting post of private secretary to the new lord deputy of Ireland, Lord Grey. This meant real action, for Spenser accompanied his employer on campaigns and was present at the bloody slaughter of the Spaniards at Smerwick in 1580. Grey always took good care of his subordinates; and when he was recalled to England in 1582, Spenser had lined his nest so well with choice bits of patronage that he decided to stay in Ireland. A series of minor government positions kept him in touch with the influential men there. In 1589 his big opportunity came in the form of a three-thousand-acre grant from the forfeited estates of the rebel earl of Desmond. From then on Spenser was one of the landed gentry, one whose ability was so generally acknowledged that he was nominated to be sheriff of Cork in the dark days of the Tyrone uprising in 1599, the year of his death.

Such a career would seem to leave little time for the writing of one of the world's longest poems. It is the crowning achievement of Spenser, as of Shakespeare, that among the difficulties of a practical career of another sort he could make a place for the creation of a body of poetry so rich and varied in its interpretation of human nature that it stands as one of the chief glories of English literature. We may well ask what kept him at this lonely and unending task year after year, far from publishers and patrons. Was it to create picturesque and ornamental tales of a bygone chivalric age? Hardly. We cannot imagine the Spenser who emerges from modern biographical research spending hours of labor for such an end. The poem was to make his fortune at court, but it was to make it as the supreme interpretation of his own age, not as amusement for an idle hour. Queen Elizabeth, who rewarded him with an income of £50 a year, had no idle hours.

That Spenser wrote "escape literature" in his epic is a commonly stated and a very pernicious error. No man of his time touched the life of his age at so many points—intellectual, religious, political, military, and geographical—and no man wrote about it so consistently in a creative form. His first work, the *Shepherds' Calendar*, contained powerful criticism of the abuses in the English church. His "Mother Hubberd's Tale" attacked the political power of the Cecil family in no uncertain terms and was suppressed by the government. His attacks on Mary, queen of Scots, in the *Faerie Queene* finally called forth an official protest through diplomatic channels by her son James. In fact, Spenser's own explanation of his purpose in the latter poem, expressed in the prefatory letter to Raleigh, is that he wished to illustrate the character of "a gentleman or noble person" engaged in the conduct of life. His contemporary, John Lyly, had written a best-seller called *Euphues* to provide his readers with a model of high-society manners and conversation. Spenser had the nobler aim of providing persuasive examples of the highest virtues and abilities in action.

Introduction

As Spenser surveyed his world, he was well aware that Luther and Calvin had shattered beyond repair the old unity and authority of the medieval church, that Machiavelli and his school had driven good faith out of the theory as well as the practice of politics and international relations, and that the explorers and scientists were supplanting the tight little Ptolemaic system with a new heaven and a new earth. To his mind it was evident that truth could no longer be taught by dogmatic ecclesiastical statement of doctrine. Before Luther and Calvin one could write a great moral drama like *Everyman* and end it effectively with a simple representation of the sacraments of the church. Chaucer, ending the woes of Troilus and his great love, flies up to heaven with his hero's liberated soul and beseeches us to join him in rejecting this world and in contemplating the wonder of the Trinity. Neither of these attitudes was any longer possible for a Protestant Elizabethan. The Church of England had banished the warm mysticism of the Roman church along with its belief in the effectiveness of ecclesiastical machinery; as for rejecting the vanities of the world, only the most extreme Puritans did it with any sincerity. The emphasis was on this world. Spenser's fairy queen, to whom all the virtues owe allegiance, is glory, not the queen of heaven. Yet the Elizabethans believed none the less firmly in God and the reality of spiritual values. To the dying Doctor Faustus in Marlowe's play "Christ's blood streams in the firmament," and Raleigh's religious poems have the ring of real conviction. The Elizabethans had to be shown virtue in action rather than to be told dogmatically about its importance. Sidney assures his readers in the *Defense of Poetry* that poetry is superior to philosophy because it does this. In other words, they could and did accept most of the ideals of medieval Christianity—with the exception of monasticism—but they insisted that they be expressed in literature in secular terms. Before subscribing to any doctrine of the vanity of the world they wanted to be shown the glory of it from a high mountain.

For this task Spenser was peculiarly well fitted. His early life and his first literary works show him to have been a serious-minded youth with definite religious leanings and a desire to criticize society from the point of view of Christian ethics, yet he gave up what was obviously a chance to enter the church with strong episcopal backing in order to try his hand at court life and politics under the earl of Leicester. Then came his Irish experiences of life in the raw: the slaughter of the Irish rebels, the factions and backbitings of Elizabeth's administrators in Dublin and Munster, and the establishment of his own fortunes as a public official and a landholder. That his poetic faith and his ideals of life were tough enough to withstand these changes and buffetings is one important measure of his stature as a man. That his poetic art continued to grow and deepen is a tribute to its power and reality. It cannot be too often insisted that the *Faerie Queene* is not the dream world of a recluse. It is Spenser's attempt to state in secular terms and with all the glowing colors of the Renaissance a program of Christian humanism, an appeal to his countrymen to create an England in which heroic virtues would bring a closer approach to the Kingdom of God on earth. Yet one realizes with something of a shock that not only in the pursuit of the virtue of holiness but equally in the pursuit of all the other virtues the church as an institution plays no part in the *Faerie Queene*. In the whole poem there is no picture of a Christian church or of organized Christian worship. The sacraments of baptism and holy

Introduction

communion are symbolically mentioned, but no hero receives these sacraments or speaks of receiving them. Spenser seeks to arouse enthusiasm for Christian ideals not through the church but through the experience of life.

The place of the *Faerie Queene* in literature is unique. Unlike the *Odyssey* or the *Aeneid* it does not tell a single story. Unlike *Orlando Furioso* it has a serious moral purpose; yet it lacks the sublimity and grandeur of the best parts of *Paradise Lost*. The secret of its true place lies in the nature of its allegory. In Milton and Vergil there are, of course, important meanings lying below the level of the narrative, but these meanings have to do with the history of Rome or the history of the world. In Spenser the meanings have to do primarily with ourselves. They are concerned with our ideals and our emotions and the ways in which the two affect each other. Although the stories are entertaining in themselves, their real significance lies in the problems in human behavior which they exhibit. In spite of an occasional woodenness of allegory, a hangover from the Middle Ages, Spenser's psychological intuition is excellent. His situations are of perennial human interest, like Shakespeare's, but they are not presented with the dramatist's purpose of compelling an immediate emotional reaction from an audience, nor are they given the complete realistic detail of the novelist in search of verisimilitude and local color. The setting of the *Faerie Queene* was just as unreal to the Elizabethans as it is to us. Spenser treats his narrative more as a speculative thinker telling stories to a group of intelligent and sympathetic listeners. "Here are some fundamental facts of human behavior I have come across," he says. "Let's see what we can make of them. What are their moral and psychological implications?"

[7]

To take these facts as Spenser gives them and to translate them into our own experience of life today is a fascinating and highly rewarding experience. And to do so increases our respect and admiration for Spenser both as a thinker and as a fellow-man who struggled with many of our problems in a period of the world's history hardly less difficult than our own.

CHAPTER II

SPENSER'S LIFE

THE most striking thing about Spenser's early life is how little we know of it, compared to the accounts we have of Marlowe and Shakespeare. That he was born in London, that his mother's name was Elizabeth, that he was in some way related to the wealthy Spencers of Althorp in Northamptonshire, we have on his own word. The rest is conjecture.

Many attempts have been made to discover Spenser's ancestry and its connection with the Althorp family. It will suffice here to say that all of them have been unsuccessful, although some of the most ill-founded, propounded by Grosart, have been incorporated into standard biographical accounts still generally read. It would be pleasant to suppose that John Spenser, member of the Merchant Taylors' Company in London, was the poet's father, but there is no proof of it. As to the Spencers of Althorp, the scarcity of male children in that line makes it necessary to go back four generations to find an eligible common ancestor; and, of course, the relationship may have been even more remote than that. The connection was perhaps through the poet's mother rather than his father; but, without any record of her maiden name, the progress of research in that direction is unlikely. The kinship, however remote, certainly existed, for the claim was made several times in the most confident manner in print. Any possibility of denial by Lady Carey and her sisters, all married to influential men, would have been fatal to Spenser's ambition to flourish at court.

Edmund Spenser and the Faerie Queene

Since parish registers were badly kept or not at all in the early 1550's, it is not surprising that we have no record of Spenser's birth. His matriculation at Cambridge in 1569 and his statement in one of his sonnets, written sometime between 1592 and 1594, that he was at that time approximately forty-one, make the period of 1551–52 a very reasonable guess. A credible tradition, going back to the middle of the seventeenth century, gives his birthplace as East Smithfield, a section near the Tower. In February, 1569, along with a number of other boys from the Merchant Taylors' School, he received an allowance from the estate of Robert Nowell for a gown to be worn at the latter's funeral. How long he had been at the school previous to this we do not know. It was a good school, and the evidence in Spenser's work of an excellent education makes it reasonable to assume that he had been in attendance since its opening in 1561. On April 28, 1569, he was on his way to Cambridge, supported by a gift of ten shillings from the fund established by the same Robert Nowell to aid poor students. This is all we know of Spenser's life before his matriculation at the university.

What sort of experience would a boy growing up in London during these years have had? Queen Mary died when Spenser was six or seven years old. Of the events of her reign he probably remembered in later life only the burning of the Protestant martyrs, memories which were reinforced later by the reading of Foxe's *Book of Martyrs* printed in 1563. We can hardly doubt that he was taken to see the procession and the pageants when the new queen entered London in November, 1558. Vivid accounts of these may still be read in Nichols' *Progresses of Queen Elizabeth*, where we learn of the giants Gogmagog and Corineus and of the series of four pageants in which "the first declared her Grace to come out of the house of unitie, the second that she is placed in the seat of government, staied with vertue to the suppression of vice; and therefore in the third the eight blessings of Almighty God might well be applied unto her: so this fourth now is to put her grace in remembrance of the state of the commonweale, which Time, with Truth his daughter doth reveal." East Smithfield was near the Tower, and the boy must have had his fill of martial pomp and ceremony, to say nothing of the trumpets and the shooting-off of guns. Besides this, it is likely that the great names and events connected with the history of the Tower were his first introduction to the romance of national antiquity which plays so big a part in the *Faerie Queene*.

To a child in a churchgoing age the most striking evidence that a new reign had begun would have been the replacing of the Latin mass by the new English prayer-book, a revision of that used in Edward's time, and the destruction of images, decorations, and rood lofts in the churches. The beginnings of the controversy over vestments and the attempts of the returned religious exiles to remodel the English church on Calvinistic lines would hardly have interested him until his arrival at Cambridge, the center of Puritan propaganda. On the other hand, it could not have been long before he began to listen with interest to the talk of his elders on the subject of the queen's marriage. Everybody was agreed that the queen must marry for the protection of the country and to provide heirs for the crown; but it made so much difference whom she married, and upon that there was no agreement. Then, too, he became almost as soon aware of that other queen, Mary of Scotland, a figure of compelling interest to a Protestant schoolboy who knew of her claim to the English throne and what it might mean if conspiracy or natural death should remove Elizabeth. When she fled before the uprising of her exasperated subjects and took shelter, which soon became imprisonment, in England in the summer of 1568 it must have seemed that her power was ended; yet the dangerous revolt in the northern counties that very autumn showed the peril of having a Catholic claimant to the throne in the country. The reality of this threat and the difficulty of doing anything about it, short of the judicial murder of a crowned head, became ever clearer to Spenser as the years of Mary's captivity rolled on; and, as the schoolboy grew into the poet, the sinister beauty of Duessa, who was to trouble and outwit the knights of Gloriana through five books of the *Faerie Queene*, began to take shape in his imagination.

That the queen of Scots was not the only threat to the Protestant regime was made progressively more evident by the steady stream of religious refugees from the Netherlands, where Philip II's Spanish government was trying to stamp out both local liberties and heretical faith. Many of these came to London, where they were allowed to have their own Calvinist congregations, a privilege not granted to Englishmen with similar views on church matters. Thirty thousand of these refugees had arrived by 1566, and still the flight continued. It was a constant reminder that the greatest military power on the Continent was only awaiting a proper opportunity, whether diplomatic or strategic, to become the instrument for re-establishing the Catholic church in England. Against Mary's plots and Philip's might there stood in the eyes of the younger generation only the gallant figure of their still unmarried queen, as she miraculously escaped one crisis after another with an inscrutably opportunist diplomacy

which baffled older heads than those of the scholars of the
Merchant Taylors' School.

Two other figures, subsidiary to the queen in the public estimation but still the subject of much talk, undoubtedly played some part in the young lad's thoughts about
great affairs. These were the dashing and magnificent earl
of Leicester, the queen's favorite, and Sir William Cecil
(later Lord Burghley), her quiet, scholarly, hard-working
secretary of state. Because his father, the earl of North-
umberland, had been in effect dictator of England during
the latter and more radically Protestant half of King Edward's reign, Leicester was regarded as the natural leader
of the Protestant reforming element in Elizabethan politics, although his own interest in religion was extremely
small. This, however, was a minor matter in the public
eye in comparison with his position as the favorite and the
possible husband of the queen. The suspiciously convenient death of his wife, the unfortunate Amy Robsart, in
1561 caused widespread scandal but did not permanently
impair his position at court. Cecil, a less known and therefore more sinister figure, was acknowledged to be the
most astute statesman in the realm, having served a successful apprenticeship in the two previous reigns. His cautious handling of his affairs during those troubled times
had already made him wealthy, and Elizabeth, who placed
her principal reliance in his counsel, added to his riches.
This affluence, no matter how much he tried to conceal it
under moderate behavior and display, was used against him
by his opponents as evidence that he had plundered the
public purse unscrupulously. His crafty, farseeing policies
were often at variance with the political opportunism of
Leicester. He favored alliances with Catholic powers; he
even favored the queen's marriage with a Catholic prince

if it would strengthen England's diplomatic position. As the watchdog of the treasury, he was opposed to war as being expensive as well as dangerous. Such policies angered the impulsive Protestant patriots of Leicester's party. The modern historian's opinion of Leicester is low, but in his own time he figured as one of the leaders of enthusiastic patriotism, a sentiment too often chafed by the devious delays of Cecil, and it is not difficult to understand how he would have had more appeal to a youngster like Edmund Spenser.

In this account of Spenser's boyhood I have been assuming what I think nobody denies, namely, that he was brought up in a Protestant family. Aside from what we may deduce from his later writings, there are two excellent proofs of this: his education in a Protestant school and his contribution in 1569, the year of his going to Cambridge, of verses to a strongly Protestant book, John Van der Noodt's *Theatre for Worldlings*. Neither of these facts tells us anything about the particular brand of Protestantism favored by his family, for the *Theatre*, although it contains a Calvinistic treatise in addition to its poetry, does not in the poetry itself inculcate sectarian doctrines. It would be of extraordinary interest if we could discover how Spenser came to be involved in the English version of this book. Van der Noodt, one of the Flemish refugees we have already mentioned, arrived in London in 1567 and probably brought with him the Dutch version of the *Theatre*, which was published by Henry Bynneman in the following year. It contained a dedication to the mayor of London, a series of epigrams and sonnets (translated from Petrarch and Du Bellay), and a religious treatise in prose. This volume was next translated into French by Van der Noodt, who seems to have been a capable linguist, and also

printed in 1568. In 1569 the English version appeared from
Bynneman's press. The dedication, in this case to Queen
Elizabeth, was composed by the author himself, the prose
treatise was translated into English by one Theodore
Roest (otherwise unknown), and the verses were translated by Spenser, although he got no credit for it in the
book. These translations, which were made from the
French version, are not beyond the powers of an intelligent schoolboy of literary taste, and the poet was at some
pains to revise them when he published them among his
own works in the *Complaints* volume twenty-two years
later. Which of these three men, Van der Noodt, Roest, or
Bynneman, knew Spenser and employed him to make the
translations? Twelve years later Bynneman printed Spenser's correspondence with Harvey, but it is more likely
that Harvey, who had already employed Bynneman as a
printer, was the one to make the deal. Spenser's own
Shepherds' Calendar had been printed the year before by a
different printer. Very likely the question will never be
answered.

As we have seen, Spenser entered Pembroke College,
Cambridge, at the beginning of the summer term in 1569.
It is useless to speculate why Cambridge rather than Oxford was chosen for his education. In any case, the choice
was a happy one in many ways. It was the university of
the great humanists of the generation just past. Sir John
Cheke, Roger Ascham, Bishop Ridley, and Walter Had-
don were still names to conjure with in England even
though the men were dead; while the statesmen Sir Thomas Smith and Sir William Cecil and the churchmen Archbishop Parker and Grindal, bishop of London, continued
the humanist tradition of service to the state. Although
academic standards in Spenser's time were distressingly

low, the university enjoyed a somewhat liberalized curriculum and was known as the home of new and radical ideas. In particular the anti-Aristotelian logic of Peter Ramus, the great Parisian scholar, and the writings of John Calvin of Geneva, founder of Presbyterianism, were very warmly received there. In other words, it was a place where, however dull the formal instruction might be, an intellectual ferment was going on. Ambitious youngsters found that traditional views were being subjected to searching and often destructive analysis.

Ramist logic, though it left its mark on the writings of many Cambridge graduates, was not a matter which aroused any official concern among the leaders of church and state. Calvinist logic was quite another thing. Calvin's views, like those of Marx today, were thought to threaten the existing regime, and their popularity at Cambridge caused constant worry to Archbishop Parker and to Sir William Cecil. The English church in those days was not the accepted fact which it became a century later. It had taken half-a-dozen changes of direction in the last generation, and its future character was at that time equally doubtful. Each group of opinion was hoping to capture the church for its own program. The queen's taste was for Catholic ritual, but her politics were of necessity Protestant. The Catholic bishops of Mary's reign had almost all refused to serve in Elizabeth's church, and the new bishops were of many shades of opinion. The most active intellects in the country favored a Calvinistic system; the queen and the bulk of the people, outside a few reforming centers, did not desire any radical changes. Furthermore, in 1569 the queen had not yet been excommunicated by the pope. This meant that her maintenance of a church not too different from the Roman system had a definite diplomatic value.

To these arguments for a cautious compromise the reformers, who were soon to be known as Puritans, opposed the force of moral enthusiasm. They envisaged a complete return to primitive Christianity, as they interpreted it, with a democratic church organization in which bishops and archbishops would have no place and in which congregations would elect their own ministers. In addition, they constantly urged the importance of preaching and objected to the ordination of clergymen not qualified to preach effectively. To this the queen, whose Tudor mind abhorred democracy and saw in preaching only an opportunity for seditious propaganda, was unalterably opposed.

Had the Church of England been at its conceivable best, these questions would still have been worth arguing about. Actually, because of the rapacity of the queen and her favorites and because of the lack of an adequate number of able and conscientious clergy, the church was in a deplorable condition and offered a broad target for the attacks of the reformers. Pastoral duties were neglected, and pluralism, the holding of several positions and their salaries by one man, was common. The theory of the church depended upon the existence of a laity thinking intelligently about doctrine and worship, yet the people were not instructed. When Puritan propagandists were able to point out these and other obvious corruptions in the actual operation of the ecclesiastical system, it was no wonder that many people felt that a change in the system itself might be desirable in order to bring about a new spirit of righteousness.

If young Spenser's own observation had not made him aware of these things before his arrival at Pembroke College, the conversation at the university would soon have brought them to his attention. It is highly significant that Thomas Cartwright's famous lectures on the Book of Acts, in which he deduced a presbyterian polity from the record of the apostolic church and severely criticized the Church of England for not returning to it, took place in the spring of 1570, that is, at the end of Spenser's Freshman year. These lectures threw the university into an uproar. Whitgift preached strenuously in reply, cautious heads of colleges protested to the government, and Cartwright's friends wrote petitions in his favor. From what we know of Spenser's early poems, written six or eight years later, it is obvious that he must have listened to these discussions with intense interest and doubtless contributed his own share to the babel of tongues in the college quadrangle.

Spenser's religious views have puzzled many students because of their apparent inconsistency and have aroused some differences of opinion among scholars. It is important, therefore, to point out that the Puritan arguments at this time were bound to appeal to the idealism of youth and its sympathy with radical reform. Although Spenser afterward became secretary to a bishop and throughout most of his life apparently found the Anglican church a satisfactory framework for the national religious life, I find no difficulty in assuming that Cartwright's demand for radical reform in the morals and government of that church found a sympathetic hearer in the young Freshman who was later to devote the first book of his great poem to the subject of holiness. In later life, complexities are better understood, and a fuller acquaintance with problems inclines men to accept compromise; evil and corruption strike us with greater force when we first become aware of them. To this moral fervor of youth the Puritan program offered an immediate answer. Destroy the tyranny and wealth of the bishops, give congregations the right to elect earnest preachers, hold out the hand of brotherhood to the Presbyterian churches of Scotland and the Continent, and the City of God will be just around the corner. These were aims to give one's life to, and the knowledge that they were politically dangerous only added to the attraction.

Pembroke College itself, although it has sometimes been described as a hotbed of Puritanism, does not appear from its choice of masters to have been especially radical. In fact, it had rather run to bishops—Ridley, Grindal, Whitgift, and Young all having held that office. Grindal, although favoring a preaching ministry, had upheld the established church and was considered so safe in his views by Elizabeth that she made him archbishop of Canterbury on Parker's death in 1575. Whitgift, who later succeeded Grindal at Canterbury, was famous for his attacks on the Puritans, and Young never showed any leanings toward the left. Young was master during all of Spenser's academic career but was absent most of the time. The senior fellow, who acted as deputy, was Thomas Nuce, the translator of the Senecan *Octavia* and therefore a person likely to encourage Spenser's ambition as a writer. Young, nevertheless, became sufficiently well acquainted with the poet so that he selected the latter as his secretary when he became bishop of Rochester in 1578.

In Spenser's Sophomore year an event of great importance in his personal life occurred. This was the election to a fellowship at Pembroke of Gabriel Harvey, who for the next ten years was his closest friend. Although he had failed in his ambition to secure a fellowship in his own college, Christ's, Harvey came to Pembroke with considerable prestige as a brilliant student and as a protégé of the distinguished scholar and statesman, Sir Thomas Smith. Harvey's aim was to be the so-called "universal man" of the Renaissance. His reading was prodigious and covered all subjects. Not satisfied with his achievements in Greek and in rhetoric—he was university professor of the latter from 1574 to 1576—he was working up an interest in civil law, to which he finally devoted himself when offered a fellowship at Trinity in 1578. He was also ambitious to follow the humanistic ideal of his patron Smith and of other great Cambridge scholars of the older generation by going into the service of the state in some capacity. To this end he cultivated acquaintances with the great on every occasion, especially with the earl of Leicester, whose patronage he seems to have enjoyed.

Here again was an influence particularly likely to affect an undergraduate with Spenser's tastes and needs. Just as Cartwright and the Puritans appealed to his moral enthusiasm, so the omnivorous learning and striking personality of Harvey appealed to his capacity for hero-worship, and the ambition of Harvey to rise in the world appealed to his need, as a poor boy, to make a career for himself. We have seen that, as a schoolboy, Spenser knew French. It is quite likely that it was Harvey, with his interest in modern literature and political theory, who led him to take up Italian. But the cause need not have been personal friendship. We have Harvey's own evidence that these were popular topics at the university. Ten years later, writing to Spenser of affairs at Cambridge, he says: "Machiavel a great man: Castilio [Castiglione] of no small reputation: Petrarch and Boccace in every man's mouth: Galateo and Guazzo never so happy: over many acquainted with Unico Aretino: the French and Italian when so highly regarded of scholars? The Latin and Greek when so lightly?" The fact remains, nevertheless, that Harvey owned a great many Italian books which he probably lent to his young admirer. It is doubtful whether Spenser ever equaled Harvey's range of interests in acquiring knowledge, but no one can doubt, after going through Harvey's letters and marginalia, that he must have tremendously stimulated Spenser's mind at a time when such an influence would bear the most fruit.

Of Harvey's all too aggressive ambition to rise in the world, both academic and courtly, much was made by his enemies in his own time and perhaps too much has been made by modern scholars. Apparently he was given to flattering his superiors, a common Elizabethan practice, and to scorning the attainments of those who were supposed to be his equals. To Spenser, a student three years younger in point of matriculation, who could not be supposed to be his equal, this side of his character would not have been evident. Harvey was undoubtedly pleased by the admiration of a gifted undergraduate and admitted him before long to real intimacy. The two of them must have often talked over their hopes and desires. It is clear that Harvey's included advancement at court. This phrase has a somewhat sordid connotation for modern readers. What we need to understand is that in general this was the only road to important government positions. We also need to remember that in the sixteenth century the divorce between the scholarly and the active life had not yet occurred. Good Latinists were in demand for secretaryships, and Sir Thomas Smith, Harvey's patron, had moved easily from classical scholarship, in which he had established an enviable reputation, to diplomacy. There was no reason why Spenser should not have regarded Harvey's wish to advance from Cambridge to Westminster as wholly admirable, and there is no doubt that by the time he received his Master's degree in 1576 he was imbued with a similar desire for his own advancement.

We now come to the most obscure period in the poet's life. From the granting of his Master's degree on June 26, 1576, to the early spring of 1578 when he became secretary to Bishop Young we know nothing with any certainty. The standard lives of Spenser make much of a supposed visit to the "north parts" of England at this time. Now that the theory of his Lancastrian ancestry has been destroyed there is no reason any longer to take seriously these attempts to translate into fact the poetical fictions of the *Shepherds' Calendar* and its commentary. The simple fact is that we do not know what Spenser did after receiving his degree. It is conceivable that he may have stayed at the university to study theology, although there is no evidence of it on the records. It would have been natural for a bishop to select a theological student as secretary. On the other hand, he may have sought employment, through Harvey's aid, with the Sidneys and the earl of Leicester. A passage in Spenser's *View of Ireland*, written in 1596, makes the principal speaker in the dialogue, who is generally taken to be Spenser himself, say that he was present at an event in Limerick in July, 1577. Since Sir Henry Sidney, Leicester's brother-in-law, was at that time lord deputy, a natural interpretation would be that Spenser was the bearer of dispatches from the earl to Sir Henry. This view of the matter would fit in with Spenser's later service with Leicester in 1579 and with his appointment to go to Ireland as Lord Grey's secretary in 1580. On the whole it seems a very reasonable conclusion.

The next ascertainable event in Spenser's life determined the nature of his first independent literary venture. This was his employment as secretary to John Young, master of Pembroke College, who became bishop of Rochester early in 1578. We cannot doubt that Spenser had been interested in writing poetry and in the religious problems of his day long before 1578, but life in a bishop's household, particularly in the household of a bishop who resided at Bromley, only ten miles from London, and who was a member of the Privy Council, would have sharpened his interest and provided him with an incentive to write with a definite audience in mind, an audience composed of his employer and the circle around him. Seven of the twelve eclogues in the *Shepherds' Calendar* refer either to the bishop or to the author's residence in Kent, and four of them are definitely concerned with ecclesiastical problems. Although the latter do not contain any attacks upon episcopacy as such, they do contain vigorous satire upon the pride and pomp of bishops and the lack of zeal among the clergy. They show Spenser boldly using poetry as a means of discussing and influencing the life of his time.

No details of Spenser's life with the bishop have come down to us. We know of it through a chance inscription in a book he gave to Gabriel Harvey. Presumably he was employed when Young took office, but we do not know when he left to go into the service of the earl of Leicester. Young was an important man and a rising one. Spenser doubtless hoped to rise with him. In what capacity? A man does not remain a secretary all his life. Spenser was a poet and, to judge from his later work, an antiquarian. As such he would have an appeal for many patrons in those days, but an episcopal patron could presumably advance him only in the church. It may be answered that service under Young, an old friend, was merely a stopgap until some-

thing better turned up; and it is easy to read the evidence
that way. Nevertheless, I think we should keep in mind
the possibility that the young poet was seriously considering the church, among other careers open to him, as a pro-
fession at this time.

The year 1579 was in many ways the most important
in Spenser's life. Early in the spring, perhaps in the preceding winter, the *Shepherds' Calendar* was finished, for the
epistle to Harvey by "E. K." is dated April 10. In December it was entered for publication on the Stationers'
Register, and the printed copies bear the date 1579. By
October 5 he had left the bishop of Rochester and was
writing to Harvey from Leicester House in London, discussing a proposed trip abroad in the service of the earl.
On October 27 he was married at St. Margaret's, Westminster, to a girl of nineteen years with the strange name
of Machabeus Chyld.

The *Calendar* requires only brief mention, as it will be
treated in a later chapter; his marriage and his relations
with the earl of Leicester must be considered more fully
here. In the *Calendar*, which was published anonymously,
the poet appears as Colin Clout, a poor shepherd. He bewails his lack of success in love, but he also objects in a
much more vigorous manner to the abuses of the Church
of England. Pride and laziness are too common; preaching
is in decay; those in high places do not set a good example.
Bishop Young and Archbishop Grindal are praised under
obvious disguises; other clerics doubtless were identified
by contemporaries. Spenser does not go so far as to wave
the red flag of Presbyterianism, but he does boldly defend
Grindal against the queen's action in suspending him for
favoring discussion meetings among the clergy.

Scholars have suspected for a good many years that

Spenser's Life

Spenser was married in the winter of 1579–80, because of certain passages in the Spenser-Harvey letters. The discovery of the documentary evidence in 1931 has led to a reconsideration of the whole matter. It now seems reasonably certain that the Rosalind celebrated as a hardhearted beauty who rejects Colin in the *Shepherds' Calendar* is a poetical projection of Machabeus Chyld and that Harvey, in his letter of April 23, 1580, refers to her change of heart and marriage to Spenser. From various passages in the poems and letters we may infer, I think, that she was a young lady of considerable wit and spirit, and she must have taught Spenser a good deal about the nature of women and the emotion of love. The only later reference to her is a line in *Daphnaida*, signifying her death shortly before 1591. She bore him a son, Sylvanus, and a daughter, Catherine. It is worth noting that what we may assume to have been the first years of strong emotional excitement in Spenser's life were also years of prolific literary planning and production. Besides the *Shepherds' Calendar*, published in 1579, he tells us that he had completed a book known as the "Dreams" (never printed), had planned the "Epithalamion Thamesis" and "Dying Pelican" and the "English Poet," and had begun the *Faerie Queene*. There is also a mysterious reference by Harvey to his "Nine Comedies" which has caused great amazement among scholars, none of whom is able to imagine Spenser as a dramatist.

Spenser's connection with the earl of Leicester was certainly an important turning-point in his life and has been the occasion in modern scholarship for one of the most brilliant theories ever put forward about him. From the more or less scholarly and clerical setting of the bishop's circle at Bromley he moved into the household of the queen's favorite, one of the most influential noblemen in

England. Foreign and domestic politics, intrigue and flattery, the theory and practice of getting ahead, surrounded him on all sides. It was an exciting life, and he writes about it to Harvey, who must have envied his young disciple, with great enthusiasm. Big names dot the page as Spenser revels in the high company he is now enjoying. It appears that there was even a wild moment when he thought of showing off in public by dedicating the *Shepherds' Calendar* to Leicester. Cautious second thoughts saved him from this bit of presumption. The dedication was shifted to the earl's nephew, Philip Sidney, then a much lesser figure in the public eye. After the *Calendar* came out, Spenser and Harvey, who corresponded frequently and met occasionally in London, began to concoct a publicity scheme to build up a demand for their respective works. This took the form of a series of letters which they would pretend were published without their permission. In these, as well as in the *Calendar*, all of Spenser's projects mentioned above were prominently discussed, and there is much talk of Harvey's great ability. But a sudden change in Spenser's life put an end to all these hopes. The letters were entered on the Stationers' Register on June 30, 1580. In August he sailed for Ireland as private secretary to Lord Grey, the new lord deputy of that turbulent country.

Why, then, did Spenser leave England in the midst of plans which apparently required his presence in London? Professor Edwin Greenlaw, in 1910, propounded the theory that Spenser's "Mother Hubberd's Tale" was a warning to the earl of Leicester that Burghley and the queen's French suitor, the duke of Alençon, would supplant him in the queen's favor if the match went through; that the queen was angered at the circulation of the poem (in manuscript, of course, since it was not published until much later) and punished the earl; and finally that the earl punished Spenser by getting him sent to Ireland as secretary to Lord Grey. The particular attractiveness of this theory was that in addition to giving a political interpretation to "Mother Hubberd's Tale" it also gave a plausible reason for the poet's lines prefixed to "Virgil's Gnat" in which he speaks of having been wronged by Leicester and complains of his suffering, which he compares to the fate of the gnat in the poem. The argument, nevertheless, overlooked several important matters of fact and is based on the rather absurd assumption that Leicester would have been so unaware of an obvious political situation that one of his young retainers had to point it out to him in a poem. The most recent special studies have not accepted so early a date for the poem and have rejected the interpretation.

The interesting questions of Spenser's relations with the earl of Leicester and of his employment by Lord Grey still remain with us. That Spenser admired Leicester and felt a sense of personal devotion to him is shown not only by the tone of the prefatory verses to "Virgil's Gnat" but even more strongly by the very moving lines of tribute to him which stand out in the general frigidity of the "Ruins of Time," published in 1591, three years after his death:

> I saw him die, I saw him die, as one
> Of the meane people, and brought forth on beare.
> I saw him die, and no man left to mone
> His dolefull fate, that late him loved deare:
> Scarce any left to close his eyelids neare;
> Scarce any left upon his lips to laie
> The sacred sod, or *requiem* to saie.
>
> He now is dead, and all with him is dead,
> Save what he in heaven's storehouse uplaid:
> His hope is faild, and come to pass his dread,

And evil men, now dead, his deeds upbraid:
Spite bites the dead, that living never baid.
He now is gone, the whiles the fox is crept
Into the hole, the which the badger swept.

He now is dead and all his glorie gone,
And all his greatness vapoured to nought,
That as a glass upon the water shone,
Which vanisht quite, so soone as it was sought.
His name is worne already out of thought,
Ne any poet seeks him to revive;
Yet many poets honoured him alive.

What it was that appealed so strongly to the young man
in his patron's character we shall never know. To modern
historians he is not a noble statesman or even a very able
one. Spenser's devotion was probably aroused by some
passing act of graciousness or some bit of practical assistance of the kind which history never records but which en-
graves itself upon the heart of the grateful recipient. He
may even have helped to make Spenser's marriage possible.

The departure for Ireland is another matter, not necessarily connected in any way with the earl of Leicester.
The latter was out of favor in 1580, and in any case it is
probable that Spenser found, after a year of running odd
jobs for ministers of state, that advancement at court was a
will-o'-the-wisp for studious youngsters such as he, no
matter how much he might yearn to follow the teachings
of Gabriel Harvey. Ireland, on the other hand, was an exciting place where fortunes might be made. At least, in
comparison to cooling one's heels at the court, it was a
place where one might see action against the rebels or the
Spanish. And if he had been at Limerick in 1577, he had
already seen action there. In Lord Grey he had a new patron who was in some ways more fitted to appeal to an

ambitious young man who had just started the *Faerie Queene* than was the splendid earl of Leicester. Grey came of an ancient noble line, he was a distinguished military leader, and he had been knighted on the field of battle for bravery. What more attractive figure can be imagined for a poet whose mind was occupied with deeds of chivalry? Furthermore, he was known to favor poets. George Gascoigne, the most prominent literary man before Spenser and only recently dead, had been patronized by Grey and had risen to royal·favor, being made one of the ambassadors to Holland in 1577. The appointment to be Grey's secretary can hardly have seemed to Spenser the dreary exile that Professor Greenlaw painted it.

From hanging around Leicester House in hope of advancement and projecting ambitious literary plans with Harvey, the change to an active life as a participator in the campaigns and administrative duties of the lord deputy must have been a striking one. In an unexpectedly different setting Spenser was getting exactly the vital contact with the world of affairs for which he had been yearning. He learned now from the inside how the contemporary political machine was run, and he observed in the field how battles were fought. Furthermore, he must have found himself exceedingly busy writing dispatches, checking accounts, and attending Lord Grey at conferences with other officials. He handled most of Grey's correspondence with Elizabeth and Burghley, whose complaints he had to answer, paid out money to messengers, copied documents, traveled with the army, and witnessed the defeat by the Irish at Glenalmure and the victory over the Spanish expeditionary force at Smerwick. It was a hard-working, strenuous life, but it was history in the making. We may easily imagine that at this time he did not get on with the

Faerie Queene very fast. As for his other projected publications, they seem to have disappeared completely. Probably as time went by and he found no convenient opportunity to send them to the press he either lost interest in them or incorporated the materials in one way or another into the *Faerie Queene* and the *Complaints* volume of 1591.

Spenser also found that life in Ireland could be profitable as well as exciting, a comforting discovery for one who was recently married and just entering upon fatherhood at this time, his son Sylvanus having been born sometime in 1580. A lord deputy in Ireland had many ways of improving the lot of his subordinates by finding sinecure posts for them and by dividing the spoil from the constant succession of attained estates of Irish rebels. In 1581 Spenser received an appointment to the lucrative position of clerk to the Chancery for Faculties, which he continued to hold for seven years, the duties being probably mostly performed by a deputy. In the same year he acquired and then resold to one Richard Synot the lease of the abbey, castle, and manor of Enniscorthy in County Wexford; and in the following year he acquired from a forfeited estate the lease of a house in Dublin. The latter may have been for his own use. If so, he evidently did not live in it for long, since on August 24, 1582, he leased New Abbey in County Kildare, where the records show him to have resided for the next two years. That he was by now regarded as a person of some consequence is shown by his appointment in 1583 as one of the commissioners for musters in that county.

This change to a settled domicile in the country was doubtless the result of Grey's recall to England in the late summer of 1582. With that event Spenser's necessity to attend his patron upon journeys through Ireland and at public business in Dublin came to an end. Much as he admired Grey, there was nothing to be gained in returning to England with him, and Spenser was already establishing important connections in his new home.

It is probable that in these two years he found some leisure to continue the *Faerie Queene*. In 1584 he seems to have moved again, for evidence in connection with his lease of New Abbey shows that he paid no rent after his appointment as Lodowick Bryskett's deputy in the clerkship of Munster in that year. Just where his family resided from then until his settlement at Kilcolman is not known. The council for Munster did not meet in any one place permanently but alternated between the important towns, such as Cork, Clonmel, Youghal, and Limerick. We know that in 1586 Spenser was made a prebendary of Effin, which is only twenty miles from Kilcolman, but we have no evidence that he occupied that estate until 1588.

What sort of literary society could Spenser have enjoyed during his first four years in Ireland? The most distinguished literary man in Dublin was the secretary of state, Geoffrey Fenton. He was a man of travel and culture, whose fame as a writer had been securely established by a number of important translations from the Italian. Although Spenser must have known him well enough in an official way, Fenton's opposition to Lord Grey made it unlikely that there would be any intimate association. There are no references to him in Spenser's poems. On the other hand, another translator from Italian works, Lodowick Bryskett, is named at least twice in the poems and had, as we have just seen, important business connections with Spenser also. As an old friend of Sir Philip Sidney—he had accompanied him on his European tour in 1572–74—he was probably well known to Spenser already, and there is no doubt that he was his most cherished literary companion. Not only is he mentioned by name in the *Amoretti* and by pseudonym in *Colin Clout's Come Home Again*, but he also received the signal honor of having two of his poems on the death of Sidney printed with Spenser's own tribute at the end of the latter volume. Bryskett, in his turn, introduced Spenser in a highly complimentary fashion into a passage in the preface to his *Discourse of Civil Life*. This preface, which describes a gathering at his cottage near Dublin, gives as good an idea as we can get of the best literary and intellectual life to be found there. At this house party, possibly imaginary but at least entirely composed of men who were in Ireland in the early eighties, there were present, besides Spenser and Bryskett, the following gentlemen: Archbishop Long; two lawyers, George Dormer and Sir Robert Dillon; four military men, Christopher Carlile, Nicholas Dawtrey, Warham St. Leger, and Thomas Norris; and one apothecary (in those days a medical practitioner), Thomas Smith. These were all educated professional men with an interest in philosophy and letters, but only Spenser, Carlile, and Bryskett were writers. They were discussing moral philosophy when Bryskett tells us that he called upon Spenser to define and explain the moral virtues. Spenser excused himself by saying that he was treating them in his unpublished *Faerie Queene* and suggested that Bryskett read a portion of his dialogue, also unpublished. Obviously the whole point of the introduction is to lead up gracefully to the author's own translation from the Italian. Nevertheless, we may accept it as a picture of the type of intellectual society available to Spenser in Dublin. The encouragement of such men and their interest in the *Faerie Queene* must be taken into account as a favorable element in Spenser's Irish life. Too often it is assumd that he was living in a barbarian wilderness, a view which he sometimes adopted himself when seeking advancement at the English court.

As deputy clerk of the council of Munster, Spenser performed duties not unlike those he had learned under Lord Grey. Munster, which does not appear on most maps today, was roughly the southern quarter of Ireland. It was a large district, of great military importance because of its direct exposure to Spanish invasion, and was full of rebellious and only partly subdued natives. The president, Sir John Norris (later his brother, Sir Thomas), was therefore an experienced commander. He spent much of his time in expeditions about the country, upon which his clerk was expected to attend him, as well as to the sessions of the Irish parliament in Dublin. In this way Spenser added greatly to his knowledge of Irish geography and of military affairs. What is important for us to remember is that neither as secretary nor as clerk did he sit in an office with telephones and typewriters like a modern whitecollar worker. His job was active enough and not seldom strenuous.

Spenser's connection with the Norris family was not new at this time. As early as 1569 he had carried dispatches for Sir Henry Norris, father of John and Thomas, from Tours to London. Thomas, whom Spenser knew much more intimately than his older brother, had been a captain under Lord Grey in 1580 and is mentioned by Bryskett as a member of the literary group who met at his cottage near Dublin. Like Spenser he was a university graduate as well as a man of action, having received the Bachelor's degree from Magdalen College, Oxford, in 1576. John Norris was sent over as president of Munster in July, 1584, but was recalled for service on the Continent in May, 1585, leaving Thomas in his place as vice-president.

One of the principal problems which faced the council of Munster at this time was the disposition of the lands confiscated from the earl of Desmond. It was planned to distribute these among English courtiers and officials with the idea that they in turn would undertake to populate them with English settlers. Hatton and Raleigh received huge seigniories, and Thomas Norris himself acquired a large estate at Mallow. In these troubled waters Spenser proceeded to fish with considerable success. Although himself a person of no importance in the eyes of great government officials in London, he had the advantage of being on the spot and in close touch with Thomas Norris, who was the chief commissioner for these lands. The story of Spenser's acquisition of the three-thousand-acre estate of Kilcolman is a complicated one, not easily cleared up at this late date. The estate was assigned to Andrew Reade, of Faccombe in Hampshire, on March 14, 1587, but in May, 1589, we find Spenser stating that he was actually in possession of the land, having agreed to give it up if Reade should occupy it before Whitsuntide of that year. In the meantime trouble was developing with a local Irishman, Lord Roche, who entered legal suit to gain possession of the estate, maintaining that it had not properly belonged to Desmond but was part of his own inheritance. He accused Spenser of making corrupt bargains with persons falsely pretending title to the land. In spite of all this Spenser took possession of Kilcolman in the autumn of 1588, if not earlier, and became legal owner in May, 1589, through Reade's failure to appear. As to Roche, whether or not his claim was valid, he had little chance against an Englishman who was

a personal friend of the chief commissioner. Spenser re-
tained possession of the estate.

Kilcolman was an excellent location for the poet at this
time. A few miles north of Norris' estate of Mallow on
the Blackwater, it was also not far from Youghal, where
both Raleigh and Norris had houses, and from Cork, where
his friend William Lyon, once chaplain to Lord Grey,
resided as bishop of the diocese. Since Raleigh was in
Ireland in 1588 acting as mayor of Youghal, he must have
had many meetings with Spenser before they left together for England in October of the following year. These
meetings Spenser has described in a passage in *Colin
Clout's Come Home Again* which shows his delight in the
pleasant scenery surrounding his new home:

> One day, quoth he, I sat, as was my trade,
> Under the foot of Mole, that mountain hoar,
> Keeping my sheep amongst the cooly shade
> Of the green alders by the Mulla's shore:
> There a strange shepherd chanced to find me out,
> Whether allured with my pipe's delight,
> Whose pleasing sound yshrilled far about,
> Or thither led by chance, I know not right:
> Whom when I asked from what place he came
> And how he hight, himself he did ycleep
> The shepherd of the ocean by name,
> And said he came far from the main-sea deep.
> He, sitting beside me in that same shade,
> Provoked me to play some pleasant fit,
> And when he heard the music which I made,
> He found himself full greatly pleased at it:
> Yet aemuling my pipe, he took in hond
> My pipe before that aemuled of many,
> And played thereon, for well that skill he conned,
> Himself as skilfull in that art as any.
> He piped, I sung; and when he sung, I piped;
> By change of turnes each making other merry,

Edmund Spenser and the Faerie Queene

Neither envying other, nor envied,
So piped we, until we both were weary.

In other words, Spenser and Raleigh read each other's poetry and were mutually pleased. The poem goes on to say that Raleigh, having encouraged Spenser to present his epic to the queen, took him across the sea to England.

Presumably they arrived at court some time in November, 1589, for the first three books of the *Faerie Queene* were already in the hands of the publisher, William Ponsonby, and entered on the Stationers' Register by December 5. Before this Spenser had read part of his poem to the queen and received permission to dedicate it to her. The book appeared in the spring, with a last-minute letter to Raleigh, dated January 23, explaining the plan of the work. The queen's pleasure had taken concrete form in the promise of a pension. While waiting for this to be confirmed by the treasury in a legal patent, Spenser had time to look about him and enjoy his first visit to London in ten years.

Many things were changed since 1580, especially among Spenser's old friends. Leicester and Sidney, once the center of his thoughts, were dead. Sidney's widow had married the earl of Essex, and to the latter as well as to Raleigh, Spenser now looked for patronage. Both were frequent recipients of the queen's uncertain favors, but both had to reckon on the opposition of Burghley, who continued to receive the queen's political confidence. Spenser also appears to have cultivated the acquaintance of Sidney's sister, the countess of Pembroke, who now figured as an important patroness of the more high-brow writers.

It is often said that Lord Burghley opposed Spenser's pension and reduced the amount of it before issuing the

[36]

patent. This may have been true, although our evidence does not go beyond rumors, yet we cannot doubt that Spenser's antipathy to him, boldly expressed several times in his poems, was more deep-seated than a quarrel over money. In early life Spenser would have thought of him as the worldly-wise opponent of enthusiastic reformers and patriots, later as the bar to Leicester's complete ascendancy at court, and finally as one whose niggardly and cautious policy was responsible for Lord Grey's ignominious recall from Ireland. That he now found him unmoved by great epic poetry and unwilling to give ample financial recompense to its author only added new fuel to an old flame. Whatever the reasons, there is no doubt of the fact that in a volume entitled *Complaints*, published early in 1591, he expressed in transparent allegory his opposition to the most powerful of Elizabeth's advisers. Whether he underrated Burghley's power or was merely reckless is hard to say; but here again, as in the *Shepherds' Calendar*, we see that the possibility of dangerous consequences did not deter him from defending his friends and expressing his own political views in his poetry.

In the meantime, what was Spenser doing during the rest of 1590 while waiting for the official grant of his pension? Aside from the publication of the *Complaints* and of another volume entitled *Daphnaida*, we have no evidence at all, but a number of reasonable conjectures can be made. We may feel sure, I think, that he made a visit to Cambridge to look up old friends, especially Gabriel Harvey, who had contributed a set of commendatory verses—unusually good for him—to the *Faerie Queene*. Second, it is obvious from the dedications of the poems in the *Complaints* that he had been paying his respects to his wealthy cousins, the Spencers of Althorp, and was missing no opportunity to strengthen that somewhat distant relation-ship. This was especially true of Elizabeth Spencer, now Lady Carey, to whom he addressed one of the dedicatory sonnets attached to the *Faerie Queene* as well. Through them he probably met Erasmus Dryden, whose grandson reported him to have been a friend of Spenser, for the Drydens were related to the Spencers by marriage. It is also likely that through them he made the acquaintance of another relation-by-marriage, Elizabeth Boyle. Elizabeth later moved to Ireland, where she became Spenser's second wife in 1594.

Finally, it is safe to place in 1590 Spenser's visit to Hampshire reported by Samuel Woodford, a minor Hamp-shire poet, to John Aubrey, the biographer. There were excellent reasons why he should have gone there at this time. Andrew Reade, the original grantee of Kilcolman, lived at Faccombe in the northwest corner of the county, and there were doubtless business details to be settled, for we know that the final deed was not executed until October 26 of this year. Also, Sir Henry Wallop, an im-portant Irish official, one of the commissioners for the Munster lands, and a good friend of Spenser and Bryskett, was on an extended visit to his family estate at Farley Wallop, ten miles' ride from Faccombe. And Spenser may have visited Sir William Kingsmill at Sidmonton, halfway between the two, for Thomas Norris had married his daughter. Woodford also told Aubrey that Spenser com-posed some of his poetry in Hampshire. If the visit took place, as we assume, in 1590, then the poems in question were some of those contained in the *Complaints* or else the elegy *Daphnaida*, written on the death of Douglas Howard, who died on August 13.

These two volumes formed Spenser's principal literary

activity during his English visit. Two things are of immediate interest about the *Complaints:* its attacks on Lord Burghley and the fact that almost all its parts are dedicated to ladies of Elizabeth's court. If the author hoped that the latter would serve in any way to mitigate the effects of the former, he was mistaken. The copies of the book were soon "called in," that is, confiscated from the booksellers, and several writers in the next decade have left us passages testifying that the book got its writer into trouble. Luckily the attacks were not discovered until after the patent for his pension had been issued. From the literary point of view the contents must have been a disappointment to readers who purchased it because they had enjoyed the *Faerie Queene.* With the exception of "Mother Hubberd's Tale," a brilliant satire on the clergy and the court (including Burghley), they are either translations or not very different original compositions of a lugubrious and high-brow sort. Only at the memory of the earl of Leicester, in the "Ruins of Time" and the dedication of "Virgil's Gnat," does the poet break the bonds of artificiality and make us aware of his real power. The type of poetry he is essaying was out of date in 1591 and betrays his long absence from London.

In *Daphnaida*, a pastoral elegy, Spenser was on the safe ground of an established classical form particularly congenial to him and, moreover, was imitating one of the minor masterpieces of his beloved Chaucer. The result is a triumph of mood and style, not without genuinely moving passages. It was written to console Arthur Gorges, the bereaved husband, to whom Spenser speaks in the dedication to the marquesse of Northampton of bearing particular good will. He was the son of Raleigh's cousin. One stanza of this poem is of special importance to biographers because the poet says that "like wofulnesse" has given him cause to sympathize. It would seem that the death of his own wife must have been recent.

The dedication just mentioned was dated January 1, 1591, close to the end of Spenser's visit. He had already received the official grant of Kilcolman, and on February 25 his pension was issued for the sum of £50 annually, not a bad reward for a man already in possession of a deputy clerkship, a prebend, and an estate of three thousand acres. Early in March the *Complaints* appeared in print, and it is possible that he was already on his way to Ireland by the time Burghley discovered the satire on himself and stopped the sale of the book. We do not know how soon this took place.

Apparently one of the first things the poet did after inspecting his estate and reporting back for duty to the council of Munster was to begin a poem to Sir Walter Raleigh called *Colin Clout's Come Home Again.* This poem reveals much about Spenser's state of mind. Although not published until 1595, the dating of the dedication from Kilcolman on December 27, 1591, shows that an early version was complete at that time; and the later additions, so far as they can be identified, are only details. In the first place, the title itself is significant. Ireland is now "home," rather than a savage wilderness. The poet speaks with obvious pleasure of the delight he takes in the neighboring rivers and mountains, making up a charming little myth about them to embellish his work. In regard to the English court he is of two minds, as indeed he had been in "Mother Hubberd's Tale." When he thinks of it as the symbol of the greatness of England and the glory of Elizabeth, he feels that "all good, all grace there freely

[40]

grows"; but when he thinks realistically of his own experiences and observations, he says:

> "It is no sort of life
> For shepherd fit to lead in that same place,
> Where each one seeks with malice and with strife
> To thrust down other into foul disgrace,
> Himself to raise; and he doth soonest rise
> That best can handle his deceitful wit."

It is better to return to his estate in Ireland than to learn repentance too late in London. The poem, however, does not end on this subdued note but on the ecstatic praise of ideal love and of his mistress Rosalind. Although for poetical purposes she is still the Rosalind of the *Shepherds' Calendar*, for Colin Clout is still the Colin of that poem, yet she obviously stands for his new love, Elizabeth Boyle. The death of his first wife, who was probably the original Rosalind, is again referred to in lines 88–91.

One more event of Spenser's visit to London must be mentioned, since it resulted in the writing of one of his most popular works. The publication of Sidney's sonnet sequence, *Astrophel and Stella*, in 1591 was a literary sensation. Englishmen had written sonnets before this but never sonnet sequences with narrative and character interest added. Specimens of the work must have been known to Spenser before publication—he moved in the right circles for this—and he, along with most of the contemporary poets, began to imitate them. With characteristic technical artistry he invented a new variation of the English rhyme scheme, three linked quatrains and a final couplet, which he used to express with exquisite beauty of phrase the conventional Neo-Platonic courtly love of the Renaissance. The series, begun in London, undoubtedly contains sonnets addressed to his principal patroness there, his relative Lady Elizabeth Carey. In its final form, nevertheless, it appears to record his courtship of Elizabeth Boyle, being published in 1595 in the same volume with the wedding ode he wrote for her.

The years 1591–95 were probably the happiest in Spenser's life. Having at last abandoned the hope of preferment in London, he returned to Kilcolman and found it good. He already had in Ireland a respectable position and powerful friends; from his English visit he brought back the public acknowledgment that he was the greatest living poet of his country, the spiritual descendant and successor of the great Chaucer. He now settled down to improve his estate and finish the *Faerie Queene*. The speed with which he completed the next three books shows how favorable were the conditions of his life at this time. It had taken him ten years to write the first three, but the second instalment was done, in first draft at least, in four. Under more affluent circumstances and with the cares of a landlord upon him, the deputy clerkship became irksome, and in 1593 he relinquished it. Thus, after thirteen years of public service in Ireland, Spenser became an independent man, one of the landed gentry.

During this prosperous period occurred the poet's second marriage. From the *Epithalamion* and its publication in 1595 we can be reasonably sure that this took place on June 11, 1594. Elizabeth Boyle, who was won with some difficulty, if we are to accept the language of Spenser's sonnets as fact, was certainly born before 1582, for her father died in that year. On the other hand, evidence in a later lawsuit shows that she was not over twenty at the time of her marriage. She was the daughter of Stephen Boyle of Braddon, Northamptonshire, and was in some way related to Richard Boyle, later the earl of Cork.

Her brother Alexander migrated to Ireland and doubtless took her with him, but there is no evidence as to when they arrived. It is thought that they may have lived at Kilcoran, near Youghal. After Spenser's death in 1599 she remained in Ireland and was married twice more. To Spenser she bore one son, Peregrine. From this account it can be seen that we know very little about Elizabeth Boyle and practically nothing about her previous to her marriage. In spite of the remarks about pride in the sonnets—remarks more suitable to Lady Carey—it is impossible to suppose that in 1594 she was superior to Spenser in either wealth or social position. Her famous, and probably distant, relative Richard Boyle was not raised to the peerage until after 1600.

In spite of our lack of external evidence, Spenser's works themselves bear eloquent testimony to her influence on him. His devotion to her is recorded not only in the sonnets of his *Amoretti* but also in a highly emotional passage in *Colin Clout* (ll. 464–68). It must also be the poet's bride who is deified in that passage of ecstatic beauty in the sixth book of the *Faerie Queene* where she appears as a fourth to the three Graces to whom Colin is piping.

> She was to weete that jolly shepherd's lasse,
> Which piped there unto that merry rout,
> That jolly shepherd, which there piped, was
> Poore Colin Clout (who knows not Colin Clout?)
> He piped apace, whilest they him daunst about.
> Pipe, jolly shepherd, pipe thou now apace
> Unto thy love, that made thee low to lout:
> Thy love is present there with thee in place,
> Thy love is there advaunst to be another Grace.

Finally, his love for her is forever enshrined in that most charmingly personal and most beautifully finished of all wedding odes, the *Epithalamion*. One would like to know more about a girl who could make such a deep impression upon Spenser at the height of his poetical power and worldly success. He was no mere sentimentalist; he had been married before and had seen a great deal of life, including all the famed beauties of the court. Much as the thought of Spenser's first love, who gallantly went to Ireland with him and died before the hour of his triumph came, stirs our imagination and warms our hearts, it must be admitted that it was reserved for Elizabeth Boyle to inspire many of the most glorious outpourings of his genius.

In the summer of 1594 Spenser was at the peak of his career. Happily married and enjoying an increased leisure from the relinquishment of his clerkship, he began to prepare a new set of works for publication. His sonnets, entitled *Amoretti*, and his *Epithalamion* were sent to London in the autumn. Ponsonby entered them on the Stationers' Register on November 19 and brought them out in a single volume in the spring with a dedication, signed by himself, to Sir Robert Needham, a young Shropshireman who was seeking his fortune in Ireland. It does not appear that Spenser had anything to do with this dedication. Probably at the same time he sent over the manuscript of *Colin Clout's Come Home Again*, for it, too, was printed by Ponsonby with the date 1595 on the title-page. In the meantime we may suppose that Spenser was busy putting the final touches on the fourth, fifth, and sixth books of the *Faerie Queene*. We know from his eightieth sonnet, probably written in the spring of 1594, that six books were then finished. There must have remained much revision and polishing to do, for it was not until January 20, 1596, that the manuscript was entered on the Register in London.

Partly for this purpose Spenser had undertaken his

second trip to London. The *Faerie Queene* was too important to be corrected in proof by Ponsonby; the author
wished to be on hand for that important task himself. We
know, however, that he had another purpose in mind.
Because of a loan made by her father's executors, his wife
and her brothers had never received the full amount of
their inheritance. Failing to recover this by friendly means,
they entered a legal suit in London on November 20,
1596, in which Spenser's name was joined with his wife's.
This business may have kept him in London until after
Easter of 1597. While there, again he wrote and published
several works.

On the first of September he dedicated jointly to the
countesses of Cumberland and Warwick a volume called
Four Hymns. With misleading simplicity he says that the
first two hymns, written in his youth on love and beauty,
had been displeasing to these austere ladies, who wished
him to "call them in." Being unable to do so, he sought to
amend matters by writing two others in praise of heavenly
love and heavenly beauty "in stead of those two Hymnes."
This sounds dutifully submissive until we discover that
the offending hymns on earthly love and beauty appear in
the volume along with the spiritual ones. We have no
evidence except this very strange dedication, which hardly
inspires implicit belief, that the first two poems really
were early work, and many scholars believe they were all
written with intentional parallelism in 1596. Taken together, they express a Christian Neo-Platonism quite characteristic of Spenser's later work.

The wedding of the two daughters of the earl of
Worcester took place at Essex House in London on
November 8. For this occasion Spenser wrote the *Pro-*

thalamion, probably at the request of his patron, the earl of Essex. This is a showpiece of considerable splendor, in which the praises of London and the Thames River are combined with compliments to the families who are being allied in marriage. The whole ode is in the poet's most melodious and decorative style. That it gave great satisfaction and that Spenser was well paid for it cannot be doubted.

A more serious work in prose, on a topic of great practical importance to himself as an Irish landholder, was his *View of the Present State of Ireland*. This was written sometime during his visit, probably in the spring of 1596. It contains an able analysis of the troubles of the English administration and gives practical advice for remedying them. Spenser's long years of service as a government official thus bore fruit in what is now regarded as one of the ablest of the many plans drawn up for this purpose in Elizabeth's reign. He saw clearly that the attempt to combine the medieval, almost primitive, clan organization of the native Irish chiefs with a secure and efficient Tudor bureaucracy was doomed to failure. A complete overthrow of the Irish feudal system was necessary if the English were to retain peaceful control, and Spenser advocates this step at whatever cost in bloodshed and devastation. Although cast in literary form as a dialogue, the *View* was meant primarily for the perusal of government officials in London and for the queen. A copy of it came into the hands of the printer Matthew Lownes, who in 1598 entered it on the Stationers' Register. Apparently he was not allowed to print it, for the first edition did not appear until 1633, long after the author's death.

After Spenser's return to Ireland in 1597 little is

known of his life. The date of his son Peregrine's birth is not known. We have evidence from a lawsuit of 1622 that Spenser had made provision for this second son by the purchase of land in Renny in the county of Cork. This agrees with other evidence showing that Sylvanus inherited Kilcolman. Apparently little more progress was made on the *Faerie Queene*. Two additional cantos turned up eventually and were printed in the 1607 edition of the poem. It is unlikely that any important amount of it was lost.

In August, 1598, Tyrone's rebellion broke out in the north, and in October there was an uprising in Munster. In the midst of these critical events it is significant of the respect in which Spenser's abilities were held that he was recommended for sheriff of the county of Cork in an official letter sent to the lords justices of Ireland on September 30. It does not appear that he ever held this office. Things were happening too fast in Munster. Town after town fell. Thomas Norris, the president, had inadequate troops for defense. His own estate as well as Spenser's was captured, and soon the English were taking refuge in Cork. From Cork, Spenser was sent on December 13 with dispatches for London, which we know reached there about the twenty-fourth. He died on January 13, 1599, in King Street, Westminster. The cause of his death is unknown. Whether or not he died in poverty, a question which has been much debated, is unimportant, since after the rebellion was suppressed his widow regained his estates and was well taken care of by her powerful relative, Richard Boyle, soon to become the earl of Cork.

Thus ended with tragic suddenness the career of the universally acknowledged master of Elizabethan poetry. What became of his literary remains has never been discovered. Except for the "Mutability Cantos," published without explanation in 1609, we might suppose them all to have perished in the burning of Kilcolman by the rebels. At any rate their disappearance has saved us from witnessing the turning-out of the poet's wastebasket by critics and scholars. Our opinion of Spenser rests, as it should, upon completed pieces of work. The accident of his death did no damage to his fame.

CHAPTER III

SPENSER'S POETIC METHOD

(The Shepherds' Calendar)

MENTION has already been made in the preceding chapter of the _Shepherds' Calendar_ as Spenser's first complete work, a work in which he boldly used poetry as a means not only to express beauty and to seek literary fame but also to express his opinion about current political and religious problems. It is not a book much read today, for it belongs to a disused branch of poetry, the pastoral, and is written in an artificially archaic style. For this latter characteristic there were some excellent reasons in Spenser's own time, but in acting upon them he did not foresee that he would be depriving the poem of most of its possible readers in the twentieth century. Nevertheless, much can be learned about Spenser's way of dealing with his poetic materials by carefully considering some aspects of it, and to do so will clear our way for an easier understanding of the _Faerie Queene_.

Because of the general and understandable neglect of the _Calendar_, some account of it is necessary here. The significance of the title is that the twelve eclogues are named after the months of the year. The weather and occupations described are usually appropriate to the several seasons, although this propriety is not carried out in detail; Spenser's main object was not verisimilitude. Colin Clout, the principal character, tells us in the first eclogue of his love for Rosalind, a theme which is repeated in the

June and December eclogues. Paralleling his love for Rosalind is his friendship with Hobbinol. In the February, May, July, and September eclogues we find allegorical presentations of the author's views on the religious situation in England. It is significant that Colin Clout does not appear in these discussions. The other five months—March, April, August, October, and November—contain miscellaneous materials, all of them, of course, presented in pastoral form: praise of Queen Elizabeth, lament for the death of a girl, imitations of Vergil and Theocritus, the present state of poetry. A tabulation of the subjects by months reveals careful arrangement for variety in the work as published, although the eclogues may have been written in quite a different order.

All this is not very exciting to us on first reading. It requires an effort of the imagination to be moved by Spenser's courage in pointing out that Archbishop Grindal was being persecuted for serving God instead of the queen. It requires both imagination and knowledge to recapture even in part the thrill of Elizabethan readers who found themselves carried away by the unmistakable music of Spenser's verse, hidden though it was under an uncouth language, after a generation of faltering tongues and metrical incompetence. Much of this is lost forever, but there are still passages of enduring beauty and of powerful satire which will reward any readers sufficiently curious to look for them.

The most obvious point to be noted is that Spenser's first work is thoroughly traditional in the larger aspects of form and content, even though new and original in details. He chose a kind of poetry dignified by the examples of Theocritus and Vergil in ancient times and of a whole row of distinguished names in the Renaissance. E. K., the anonymous editor of the first edition, says this in his prefatory letter to Gabriel Harvey. "So flew Theocritus, as you may perceive he was already full fledged. So flew Vergil, as not yet feeling his wings. So flew Mantuane, as being not yet full somd. So Petrarque, so Bocace, so Marot, Sanazarus, and also divers other excellent both Italian and French poets, whose footing this author every where followeth." The important thing to realize here is that these writers had all developed the pastoral in the direction of personal allusion and allegorical satire on contemporary problems. The normal expectation of readers in the sixteenth century was to look for applications to the real life of their own day under the cloak of simple shepherds and their songs. Furthermore, as E. K. also remarks, it was customary for poets to choose the pastoral form for their first efforts. By choosing this form, therefore, Spenser could both disarm criticism, on the one hand, and, on the other, find himself free to express his opinions about contemporary affairs.

In another way Spenser tied his work in with quite a different tradition. By his title he reminded his readers of a popular almanac known as the *Kalendar of Shepherds*, originally a French work but long domesticated in English. It was divided into months and embellished with woodcuts showing the sign of the zodiac for each month. Both of these features were imported by Spenser into his own book, and both constituted a new development in the tradition of pastoral poetry. These were not, however, the only changes Spenser made in the tradition. It had been customary for writers of Latin pastorals to imitate Vergil strictly by using the hexameter line for all the poems. Writers in the vernacular could not do this, but they usually came as close to it as they could by choosing one meter in their native language and using it for their whole series of eclogues. Spenser broke with this tradition by using a variety of meters and by introducing songs into some of the eclogues written in a different meter from the main body of the eclogue. The *Shepherds' Calendar* is indeed a great storehouse of experiments in English versification. There is also the matter of vocabulary. Vergil had written in an elegant, sophisticated diction which made no attempt to imitate the language of real shepherds, and in this he had been followed by the Renaissance writers. Spenser boldly returned to the example of Theocritus and adopted a colloquial style, artificially created out of both archaic and dialect words, to give an impression of realism. For this he was adversely criticized by Sidney in the latter's *Defense of Poetry*, but it was in line with a considerable movement among literary men in that day which aimed at restoring native English words to use and opposed borrowings from European languages or from the classics. Following this principle, the names of the shepherds are not the standard Latin ones of Renaissance tradition but are either English or French: Colin Clout, Cuddie, Willye, Piers, Hobbinol.

I have stressed this combination of convention and originality in the *Shepherds' Calendar* because it is typical of Spenser. Throughout his work we find him habitually choosing standard and approved forms of poetry and then imposing his own stamp upon them. We see it in his treatment of the epic in the *Faerie Queene* and the sonnet in the *Amoretti* no less than in the pastoral here. Being preeminently a good workman, he did not quarrel with his tools, but he made them do work they had never done before.

Equally typical of Spenser is the vigor of his attack on

the government's policy in regard to the English church. In his Cambridge days he had been exposed to powerful and persuasive propaganda in favor of sweeping reforms which would establish the presbyterian system in the Church of England instead of the episcopalian. The opening wedge was the attack on the low moral and spiritual state of the church. In the meantime Spenser had grown older and become secretary to a bishop. There is no attack on the episcopalian system in the *Calendar*, but there is plenty of attack on the lordliness and wealth of bishops and on the laziness and ignorance of priests; and this attack is pressed even harder in that part of "Mother Hubberd's Tale" which was written not long after the *Calendar*. More specific than this was his open defense of Archbishop Grindal in the May and July eclogues. Grindal had been suspended from his ecclesiastical functions by the queen because he had refused to suppress the discussion meetings which were being held by the reforming party in the clergy. Besides general praise of Grindal under the transparent allegorical name of Algrind, Spenser pointed directly to the queen as his persecutor in the fable of the eagle and the shellfish by making the eagle a female. In the September eclogue there is an attack on some unidentified enemy of Bishop Young, here called Roffy from the Latin name of his diocese (*episcopus Roffensis*); and in the February eclogue the fable of the briar and the oak certainly deals with some contemporary matter, although scholars are not agreed as to what it was. These are minor matters in comparison with the direct attack on royal interference with the church in the Grindal affair. Here Spenser showed unmistakably that he was not afraid to deal with dangerous material. Perhaps it was just as well that he published the book anonymously.

Finally there is the question of the allegory in the *Shepherds' Calendar*. The basis of Spenser's allegory here as in the *Faerie Queene* is first of all the creation of an imaginary world to shadow forth the world of reality. In this case it is the imaginary world of pastoralism, well known to all readers of the classics and therefore requiring no extra effort or build-up on the part of a Renaissance writer. In this world shepherds meet in the fields or under the shade of trees to sing of their love, to compete for prizes in piping, or to bewail their misfortunes. By convention they never do any work, although they may complain about the work they have done or are about to do. During the two centuries before Spenser a tradition had grown up of referring to real people and events under the fictitious names used in pastoral poetry, and of this tradition he makes full use. Therefore a reader approaching this poem must ask himself how he is to interpret the figures presented to him. When is he to look for relationship between the real and imaginary worlds, and how exact is this relationship going to be? It must be admitted immediately that Spenser makes use of several different levels of relationship. It must also be admitted that the notes supplied by Spenser's friend E. K. as editor cannot be used with much confidence in solving this problem. Sometimes they identify a character quite clearly for us, but at other times they are silent or confusing. From the start it is evident that Colin Clout represents Spenser himself; it is also evident that E. K. is correct when he tells us that Hobbinol represents Gabriel Harvey. Simple reversal of syllables tells us that the revered old shepherd called Algrind is Archbishop Grindal; Roffy is revealed as the bishop of Rochester by comparison with the latter's Latin title. These are what may be called absolute identifications since they are provided by Spenser himself and are universally accepted. On a different level are Cuddie, Lowder, Lobbin, Dido, Rosalind, Wrenock, and E. K. himself. All these undoubtedly stand for real people, but no direct clues are given to their identity, and scholars do not agree in their guesses. We may safely assume that they were meant to be recognized by an inner circle of Spenser's friends but not by the general public. E. K. hints that one or two other characters are real people, but I feel no confidence in his remarks on this subject when they are not supported by other evidence. It was clearly the editor's intention to whet the public interest by suggesting hidden meanings as often as possible. To this group some scholars would add several shepherds from the eclogues attacking the evils of the church. This is always a possibility, but the evidence advanced has not been very convincing. Morrel and Palinode seem to me much more like types of clergymen disapproved by Spenser than like particular individuals. Last come the purely decorative characters—Thenot, Perigot, Willye, and the rest—who were put in merely to fill out the picture and to provide interlocutors where needed.

If these conclusions are accepted, we may state with some certainty the principal things Spenser is telling us about the real world under the allegory of his imaginary world. He is first of all attacking abuses in the church and defending Archbishop Grindal. At the same time he manages to throw in a few compliments to Bishop Young, who was his employer at the time of writing. Next he is celebrating his friendship with Harvey, to whom the prefatory letter of E. K. is addressed. Balanced against the friendship theme is that of his love for Rosalind, certainly a real girl whether or not she was his first wife, as has recently been suggested. Finally, in the October eclogue, he is giving us his views on poets and poetry. Whatever other specific ends he had in mind were meant to be understood only by his intimates and not by general readers in his day or our own. It should also never be forgotten that these specific or, shall we say, practical ends were only a part of Spenser's purpose in writing. He is also creating beauty because it is in his heart and must be expressed, using words as his medium because he loves them and their music. The song in the April eclogue is not merely praise of a monarch, a potential patron. It is an enthusiastic fusion of joy in the spring with its bright flowers, exuberant national pride in a virgin queen who dazzled courtiers with her wit and her diplomatic triumphs, and living memories of that luminous world of classical myth peopled with graceful light-clad nymphs and dryads. To connect it only with the historical person of Elizabeth Tudor is to miss the whole function of poetry. Similarly, on a lower level, the incidental fables are not just disguised attack. We can feel in them the joy of a narrative artist telling a story neatly and well, putting the right word in the right place, making his points succinctly and with precision, proud of what he has learned from Chaucer.

There remains the question of the relation of the poet himself to his imaginary world. This is a particularly interesting question about Spenser because Colin Clout was adopted by him as a permanent poetical projection of himself, appearing in *Colin Clout's Come Home Again* and the *Faerie Queene* as well as in the *Shepherds' Calendar*. To what extent is Colin actually Edmund Spenser, and to what extent is he an imaginary character with freedom to do and say things not meant to represent the life of his creator? Bound up with this is the question of Rosalind,

who is mentioned by name in *Colin Clout's Come Home
Again* and, as the beloved of Colin, is apparently the
fourth Grace in the famous scene at the end of the sixth
book of the *Faerie Queene*.

In the *Shepherds' Calendar* we learn that Colin is a
southern shepherd's boy and that the shepherd's name is
Roffy. This, with the information given by E. K. that
Colin is residing in Kent, quite sufficiently establishes his
identity with the author, who at this time was secretary
to the bishop of Rochester. He is also represented as a
close friend of Hobbinol, who according to E. K. is Gabriel Harvey. The name Colin Clout is that of the principal
character in one of Skelton's savage attacks on the wealth
and pride of high church officials, especially Cardinal
Wolsey, written half a century earlier. Thus the appearance of a character by the same name in the very first
eclogue of Spenser's book was an indication to knowing
readers that satire on the abuses of the church was to be
expected. This, as we know, was true, but it is strange
that Colin himself is never the mouthpiece for the attack
nor does he appear in any of the satirical eclogues. Consequently we may note at once that he is not a complete
poetical projection of the author. What, then, is he? If we
examine the passages in which he appears and the references to him in the *Calendar*, we find that he most frequently appears as a poet, the most admired and skilful
poet in the little pastoral world of the book. He himself
sings the technically elaborate dirge for Dido; his equally
elaborate song for Queen Elizabeth and the literary tour
de force of his sestina in the August eclogue are quoted by
other shepherds. His two prayers to Pan, in January and
December, are simple metrically but extremely smooth and
effective in style. In spite of these brilliant performances,

[57]

Colin humbly disclaims any poetic skill, in words reminiscent of Chaucer's Franklin. Indeed, he refers to Chaucer several times as his model.

As befits a poet in the pastoral world, Colin is represented as disappointed in love. This was the usual thing and was expected of him. Curiously enough, none of his songs is in praise of Rosalind. We should also note that his love story is not fully told. Colin says at first only that Rosalind has rejected him. Later we learn that he had once found favor but had been replaced in her affections by Menalcas. There are no details. Although Colin does not sing songs in praise of his beloved, we are told in an interesting passage in the October eclogue that love is the inspiration for his best efforts. Cuddie says that Colin would make famous flights of poetry if he were not so unfortunate in love. Piers replies:

> Ah fool, for love does teach him climb so high
> And lifts him up out of the loathsome myre:
> Such immortal mirrhor as he doth admire
> Would raise one's mind above the starrie skye
> And cause a caytive corage to aspire,
> For lofty love doth loath a lowly eye.

Knowing that in a number of important points Colin stands for the author, we naturally inquire to what extent we are to believe that Spenser himself was actually suffering the pangs of unrequited love at the time the *Calendar* was being written. For the moment it is enough to make two observations. First, convention required Colin to be in love and unhappy. Second, we do have some evidence that Spenser was in love at this time. We know that he was married on October 27, 1579, about six months after the *Calendar* was completed but six weeks before it went to press. We also know that Gabriel Harvey evidently

supposed that Rosalind was a real person, since in his letter to Spenser on October 5 he says that the *Calendar* was
"made in honor of a private personage unknowne, which
of some ill-willers might be upbraided, not to be so worthy
as you know she is." This is certainly Rosalind, and in a
letter written the following April he quotes Rosalind directly as having said that Spenser had "all the intelligences
at his command" and as having called him "Segnior Pegaso." Consequently we must believe that she was a real
person and not a poetical fiction. If she was a real person,
the close parallelism of Colin with Spenser makes it fairly
likely that Colin's love affair was also his. Possibly the unhappy outcome was introduced as a concession to the
pastoral and Petrarchan tradition, but it is hard to avoid
the conclusion that Rosalind was a real girl with whom
Spenser was in love in the year 1578–79.

We must now follow Colin into Spenser's later works.
In the *Faerie Queene* and in the *Complaints* Spenser appeared before the world as the impersonal author, but on
coming back to Ireland in 1591 after his visit to England
he decided to write a purely personal poem describing that
event. For this purpose he returned to the pastoral form
and again made Colin Clout the principal character. From
this and from the reappearance of Hobbinol and Cuddie in
the poem we might suppose that we are back in the English pastoral world of the *Shepherds' Calendar*, but we soon
find that this is not true. In spite of the presence of Hobbinol and Cuddie, who remain as a tribute to Spenser's
enduring regard for his old friends and not as a statement
of their presence in Ireland, the shepherds are Irish shepherds (one of them, Thestylis, can be identified as Lodowick Bryskett), and the incidental mythical tale told by
Colin is laid in the Irish countryside around Spenser's

home. Again the things said about Colin are true of Spenser, this time indeed with almost complete exactness, but his doings now do not take place among rustic companions; he is telling them a story of things in which they did not share. And again we have the problem of Rosalind. As in the *Shepherds' Calendar*, she does not appear personally, but she is referred to. In a striking passage at the end of the poem she is blamed by Hobbinol for having so long scorned Colin's love. Colin defends her, saying that she is a thing celestial and divine, excelling far all ordinary shepherdesses, and blames himself for looking so high. Now to anyone familiar with Rosalind in the earlier poem this is strange language. The old Rosalind had left Colin for a rival and doubtless was very attractive, but there was no indication that she was too high for Colin to aspire to. This is the language of the *Amoretti*, written about the same time as the poem we are discussing, where Spenser in true sonnet style abases himself before the proud beauty of his lady, whose heavenly virtues are far above him. We have here a different Rosalind, belonging to a different period of Spenser's life, just as Colin himself is no longer Spenser as the secretary of Bishop Young but Spenser as the successful poet and Irish landholder. Even though the pastoral world remains in part the same, it is important to realize that the symbols have changed their values.

Colin's final appearance is in the sixth book of the *Faerie Queene*, published in 1596. Sir Calidore, the hero of this book, while in pursuit of the Blatant Beast comes upon a small community of shepherds where he is persuaded to stay and rest himself. This pastoral world is not that of either of the previous poems. No names of shepherds are repeated except that of Colin Clout, who again appears as the poet most admired by the rustics. One day Calidore,

wandering in the woods, comes upon Colin piping for the
dance of the Graces. A hundred "naked maidens lilly
white" form the outer ring, while inside it the three Graces
do honor to one maiden in the center who in beauty ex-
celled all the rest:

> She was to weete that jolly shepherd's lasse,
> Which piped there unto that merry rout,
> That jolly shepherd, which there piped, was
> Poore Colin Clout (who knows not Colin Clout?)
> He piped apace, whilest they him daunst about.
> Pipe, jolly shepherd, pipe thou now apace
> Unto thy love, that made thee low to lout:
> Thy love is present there with thee in place,
> Thy love is there advaunst to be another Grace.

In this apotheosis of Colin's beloved no name is mentioned,
which somehow seems fitting, yet I think we cannot doubt
that she is Rosalind and that Colin has finally gained her.
Since we know that Spenser married his second wife,
Elizabeth Boyle, in 1594, about the time these lines were
written, we can also hardly doubt that the fourth Grace,
who in the pastoral fiction must be Rosalind, was in real
life that Elizabeth who was the inspiration of most of
Spenser's mature work.

Colin Clout, then, is the poetical projection of Spenser
as a pastoral poet. He is not Spenser as an epic poet nor
as a philosophic poet. In so far as love is traditionally one
of the subjects of pastoral poetry, Colin is also Spenser as
a poet of love. We do not find him, however, in the *Amoretti*, for the sonnet is a courtly, not a pastoral form; nor
do we find him in the *Epithalamion*, which is too personal
for the use of any fictitious representation of the exulting
bridegroom. As a poetical figure it is obvious that Spenser
had a great affection for him. Colin Clout was his first-

born offspring of the spirit. It was as Colin Clout that he told the world of his triumphal invasion of London and the court with the *Faerie Queene*. And it was for Colin Clout that he found a place, against all likelihood, in the chivalric adventures of that epic and for whom he wrote one of the great memorable passages of his poetry. That this passage comes near the end of the last completed book of the *Faerie Queene* could not have been foreseen by the writer, but it has its peculiar fitness. Fate, which was often unkind to Spenser the man, did well by Spenser the artist.

In dealing with Colin Clout a good deal has necessarily been said about Rosalind. Since she is an important and interesting figure, it is desirable to devote some attention to her in her own right. First of all we must notice that, unlike the heroines of the *Faerie Queene*, she is a *muta persona*. She appears only once and on that occasion does not speak. Our conception of her is dependent entirely upon what Colin and the other shepherds say about her. Colin, in the first eclogue of the *Calendar*, seems to say that she lived in the neighboring town:

> A thousand times I curse that carefull hower,
> Wherein I longd the neighbour towne to see:
> And eke ten thousand times I blesse the stour,
> Wherein I sawe so faire a sight as shee.

This is confirmed by E. K.'s note on Hobbinol's remark in the April eclogue that Rosalind is the widow's daughter of the glen, in which he says that he thinks Hobbinol's statement was "rather sayde to coloure or concele the person, than simply spoken." We have already seen that in the *Calendar* she is not regarded as too far above Colin. He had once had her love, but Menalcas has cut him out. Nevertheless her beauty is still the inspiration for his poetic ambition. Of Menalcas not one detail is given, which perhaps argues for his nonexistence in real life. This, then, is the original Rosalind: a beautiful country girl, living in a small town, for whom Colin once happily wove garlands of flowers and selected the choicest fruits, who later deserted him for a rival. Her image remained as the inspiration of his verse. Her reincarnations in Spenser's later poems have already been sufficiently dealt with.

We must now examine a little more closely the question of Rosalind's counterpart in real life. Here we are immediately faced with the confusing remarks of E. K. He says first of all that Rosalind is "a feigned name, which being wel ordered, will bewray the name of his love and mistresse" but then proceeds to give three examples of this practice in other poets, not one of which is actually an anagram of the lady's real name. I therefore conclude that E. K.'s first statement cannot be taken literally. So far, at any rate, the attempts to rearrange the letters of Rosalind's name have not led to any acceptable result. E. K. later says that she is not really the widow's daughter of the glen but "a gentlewoman of no mean house, nor endowed with anye vulgare and common gifts both of nature and manners." This may be pleasant flattery, just as the other is rustic depreciation; it does not require us to assume that she was wealthy or of noble birth. The intention obviously is that the reader shall think well of Colin and Rosalind. E. K.'s statements really tell us nothing except that she was a girl of superior natural endowments and manners.

The only other contemporary evidence is that of Gabriel Harvey. His letters to Spenser, published in the summer of 1580, are somewhat better evidence than the notes of E. K., which were written for public consumption.

Nevertheless, it is well to remember that we do not have the original letters themselves. The printed version of the letters appeared well after the publication of the *Shepherds' Calendar*, and we do not know what changes Harvey may have made in preparing copy for the press. Also it is obvious that there is a good deal of joking between Spenser and Harvey in the correspondence. With these reservations, we may note that Harvey, in a Latin passage in his letter of October 23, 1579, is twitting Spenser about being in love. Here he mentions no names, but in a letter written April 23, 1580, he speaks of "gentle Mistress Rosalinde," who had once reported Spenser to have all the intelligences at his command and at another time had called him her Segnior Pegaso. The use of the adjective "gentle," although perhaps merely a courtesy title rather than a description, and the use of the possessive pronoun in the second phrase suggest excellent, if not affectionate, relations between Spenser and Rosalind, quite different from those described in the *Shepherds' Calendar*. At the end of this letter is another Latin passage in which Harvey sends his regards to Spenser's sweetheart (*corculum*) whom he calls *Domina Immerito* and *bellissima Collina Clouta*, which can only mean that she was Spenser's wife, since Immerito was the pseudonym under which he had published the *Calendar*. Of her he says: "per tuam Venerem altera Rosalindula est: eamque non alter sed idem ille copiose amat Hobbinolus." The first half of the sentence used to be translated: "through your love she has become another little Rosalind," but I follow Professor T. H. Banks's recent opinion in believing that this would hardly have been regarded as a compliment by Mrs. Spenser. He translates it as "she is an altered little Rosalind," that is, although cruel to you at the time of writing your poems she has now relented and become your wife. The rhetorical structure of the sentence seems to demand this reading, for it continues: "and not a changed but rather the same Hobbinol loves her very much." To translate *alter* by "another" in both places makes very little sense, whereas "altered" or "changed" makes very good sense and is supported by many passages in standard Latin authors. Here, then, in the same letter in which Harvey has already pleasantly referred to Rosalind, he indicates that she is now married to his friend. In that case her name was Machabeus Chylde and she lived in Westminster.

To sum up, Rosalind was, even at the most cautious interpretation of the evidence, a real girl well known to both Harvey and Spenser. One does not invent quotations from the speech of an imaginary poetical fiction. She was probably the girl Spenser married in October of 1579. Both Harvey and E. K. speak highly of her manners and intelligence. She appears to have had a ready wit and to have led her poet somewhat of a chase, but she certainly was not the unapproachable divinity of *Colin Clout's Come Home Again*. That was a later and a different Rosalind.

We have learned from this examination of the *Shepherds' Calendar* several things about Spenser's way of writing poetry which will be useful to us in thinking about the *Faerie Queene*. First, it is characteristic of him to make new and diversified use of traditional forms. Second, he likes to use an extended, flexible type of allegory in which some figures represent actual individuals in real life, some of whom will be recognized by the public and others only by a select circle; other figures represent types of men rather than individuals, and still others are merely necessary or decorative and do not represent anything in the real world. We have also found that he sometimes uses a certain figure to represent one thing at one time and another thing at a later time. He may even represent a real person, in this case himself, as one fictitious character in one eclogue but as a different character in another eclogue; for E. K. suggests to us that Cuddie, who speaks as the ambitious poet in October, is Spenser too, in spite of the fact that he and Gabriel Harvey indicate in other places that Cuddie is someone else. Finally, I think that we should recognize and accept a distinction in Spenser's allegory mentioned above. When he wanted the general reader to understand his allegory, he made it reasonably clear. The perplexing parts of his allegory are those intended only for his friends. These problems form an interesting playground for Spenser scholars, whose duty and pleasure it is to find out all that can be known about him, but the intelligent reader of today who wishes to appreciate his works should not disturb himself about these mystifications. To pay no attention to Spenser's allegory is to make him meaningless and to waste one's time, but to pay too much attention to the details of it is equally unwise because it turns one's attention away from his major ends both as a poet and as a teacher.

Before going on to apply these principles to the *Faerie Queene*, we may profitably look for a moment at the October eclogue of the *Calendar*, in which the place of poetry in Elizabethan England and the problem of the ambitious youth who wishes to be a poet are discussed. Cuddie, who plays the part of the poet here, complains that he gets no reward for his verses. Piers replies that praise and glory should satisfy him but is answered that praise will not fill an empty stomach. Piers then shifts his argument and ad-

vises Cuddie to give up simple, lowly pastoral verse and
take a martial theme:

> Abandon then the base and viler clowne,
> Lift up thyself out of the lowly dust:
> And sing of bloody Mars, of wars, of giusts.
> Turn thee to those that weld the awful crown,
> To doubted knights, whose woundless armour rusts,
> And helmes unbruzed wexen dayly browne.

> There may thy Muse display her fluttryng wing,
> And stretch herselfe at large from east to west:
> Whether thou list in fayre Eliza rest,
> Or if thee please in bigger notes to sing,
> Advaunce the worthy whom she loveth best,
> That first the white beare to the stake did bring.

> And when the stubborn stroke of stronger stounds
> Has somewhat slackt the tenor of thy string,
> Of love and lustihead tho mayst thou sing,
> And carrol lowde, and leade the miller's rownde,
> All were Eliza one of thilke same ring.
> So mought our Cuddie's name to heaven sownde.

Three things are notable in this passage. First, the poet
is advised to write about kings, nobles, and warlike deeds.
Second, there is satire on the "knights" whose armor
rusts from lack of use. Third, the poet is advised to select
the queen or some great noble (here the earl of Leicester,
as E. K. points out) as the main figure in his poem. Cuddie
replies that the age lacks not only patrons like Maecenas
and Augustus but also all the worthies who performed
deeds fit for lofty verse to celebrate. Virtue and manhood
are degenerate, and as a result poetry has degenerated
with them. Then follows a significant appeal by Piers:

> O pierlesse poesye, where is then thy place?
> If nor in prince's pallace thou doe sit:
> (And yet is prince's pallace the most fitt)

Ne brest of baser birth doth thee embrace.
Then make thee wings of thine aspyring wit,
And whence thou camst, flye backe to heaven apace.

If both patrons and worthy deeds to celebrate are lacking,
the poet must draw upon the inspiration of his own aspiring mind to lead him to that which is highest. It is here
that Cuddie bewails the lack of any such powerful inspiration and says that Colin, were he not sunk in despairing
love, might climb to that height. With a further statement
by Cuddie that, if his inspiration were only adequate, he
would try his hand at a tragedy, the eclogue ends. What
a curious unconscious prediction of the aspiring mind of
Marlowe which was to take flight in tragedy within the
decade.

This eclogue was probably one of the last to be written. If the reference to Leicester is not a late addition, it
may well be the very last. Spenser feels that his work as a
pastoral poet is completed—traditionally it was supposed
to be a proper occupation for beginners—and he is looking
around with some apprehension for fresh fields. We know
from E. K.'s remarks and Harvey's letters that he had
completed, or nearly completed, several shorter works,
the "Dreams" and the "Dying Pelican" and others, but their
titles suggest that they were not cast in the major forms.
They would not raise him so high that he might look for
a court position or a pension. By the following April the
title of the *Faerie Queene* appears in one of Harvey's letters
as an addition to the list of projected publications. Harvey
frowned upon it as an unsuccessful imitation of Ariosto,
added a sarcastic comment that it was "Hobgoblin run
away with the garland from Apollo," and recommended
that Spenser polish up his nine comedies instead. We do
not know what Harvey saw; it does not sound much like

the *Faerie Queene* as we know it, and particularly it does not sound like Book I. Whatever it was, it was suspended, like all the other projects, by Spenser's departure for Ireland three months later. By the time the first three books appeared in 1590 Spenser had found in his own life the answers to the arguments of Cuddie and Piers. He found his patron in the queen, and in Lord Grey and the Norris brothers he found knights whose armor did not rust unused. He took part with his own hand and brain in the mighty attempt of Elizabethan Englishmen to conquer and civilize Ireland.

CHAPTER IV

THE NARRATIVE POET
(Faerie Queene, III–V)

WHEN Gabriel Harvey read the specimen of the *Faerie Queene* sent him by Spenser in 1580, he could not decide what kind of work it was. In his perplexity he resorted to a characteristically sixteenth-century simile. He said it was "Hobgoblin run away with the garland from Apollo." It is very unlikely that he saw what is now Book I; in fact, his second comment, that Spenser seemed to be trying to outdo Ariosto, the most amusing of Renaissance poets, points rather clearly to an early version of some part of Book III or Book IV. The implications of the whole passage on the poem in Harvey's letter are fascinating but must not now detain us. The essential facts which come out of it are that the work was even then called the *Faerie Queene* (and therefore aimed at Queen Elizabeth as a patron), that it was an imitation of Ariosto, and that it was not sufficiently dignified and classical. The combination of Hobgoblin with Apollo suggests that mixture of medieval romance with classical myth which is so characteristic of the completed poem as we have it.

Harvey's comment was made on the first portion of Spenser's new poetical project. This project must, however, have languished for some time thereafter, for the author's two years of service as secreatry to Lord Grey would have been a serious interruption. When he took it up again, some of his ideas had changed. He was no longer the bookish former secretary of a bishop but a man who had followed campaigns in the field and sat at council tables. His purely personal gratitude to the earl of Leicester had been in large part replaced by admiration for the sterner qualities of the warrior, Lord Grey. His youthful complaint that all swords were rusting unused gave way to hero-worship in the face of his Irish experiences. He would not give up the figure of Elizabeth as the fairy queen, but he would show that true and valiant knights were doing her work. Consequently the idea of an order of Maidenhead, whose knights perform quests assigned by the queen, was adopted to accommodate Spenser's desire for a number of heroes. That this was done can be shown not only by the arrangement of the poem itself but also by the letter to Sir Walter Raleigh printed with the first three books of the poem in 1590. In this famous document he says that Arthur represents magnificence, which contains all the virtues in itself, and that the other knights represent the individual virtues.

By this time many modern readers have lost patience. Why bring in the virtues? they ask. Why does not Spenser tell us his story without preaching; and, furthermore, why does he bore us by putting the action in an imaginary fairyland? To these objections the scholar has ample enough reply. He can show that the whole tone of English education and literature in the sixteenth century was moral and religious; he can also show that the writing of a strictly historical epic was in those days so loaded with political dynamite that a remote and imaginary setting was needed. There are, however, better reasons than these. As Spenser grew to a realization of his own powers, he took for his aim the creation of a great epic for the English people, which, as he put it in the dedication to Queen Elizabeth, was to "live with the eternity of her fame." By basing his

didactic purpose

poem on the fundamental virtues of mankind he saved his heroes from the fate of being local and contemporary. Whether Sir Calidore was meant to be Sidney or Essex does not concern us much today, but as the knight of courtesy struggling with the forces of cruelty and slander in the world he is of perennial interest—and never more so than at the present moment. With Britomart's dynastical position as ancestress of Queen Elizabeth we have even less concern, but Britomart's troubles in the pursuit of true and honorable love come home with fresh force to every generation of readers.

It may be said, too, that the events of the past few years have done much to restore an interest in the open treatment of moral values in literature. We have seen with terrible clarity that evil forces of tremendous power exist in this world and cannot be subdued without heroic virtues. Archimago, Grantorto, and the Soldan do not seem so absurd to those whose dreams Hitler has haunted, nor will the Cave of Mammon seem an idle temptation to those who once thought they could buy immunity from war. These things were gruesome realities in Spenser's time as in ours, and the description of England by a statesman of his youth as "shaken by the terrible thunder of God" (*terribili fulmine tacta dei*) would apply even better to 1940. It is significant to remember that during the writing of all the early parts of the *Faerie Queene* England lived under the threat of invasion, while the argument went on at court between the interventionists and the isolationists. It was a time when men had forced upon them a re-examination of the real basis of their beliefs, traditions, and ideals. Spenser's poem deals, in narrative form, with all these things.

This concept of a great epic on the active virtues of

mankind and of Englishmen in particular drove Spenser to the creation of a new form. The simple linear plot of the classical epics would not serve to express the complexities of life as he saw it; on the other hand, Ariosto's gay disregard of a central story offered no help toward the erecting of a structure which would carry the weight of serious thought. Luckily Ariosto had popularized one idea which was essential to Spenser's purpose: the presence of a number of different heroes in the same long poem. It is probable that Arthur, whether king or prince, had nothing to do with the early idea in Spenser's mind of a poem in praise of the queen; but after the scheme of multiple heroic virtues was adopted, he must have realized that the legend of Arthur's Round Table and the great deeds of his knights formed an ideal solution to his problem. Here was a story, familiar to all readers and forming the core of British patriotism, which provided for variety of heroes and unity of purpose in one and the same framework. The fact that the sovereign of England was a queen necessitated supplanting Arthur by Gloriana, and the order of the Round Table became the order of Maidenhead; otherwise it was unchanged. Once you thought of it, it was ridiculously simple. How Spenser brought Arthur in again we shall see later.

What the structure of the poem is, will appear as we go along. What the completed whole would have been, we shall never know. Spenser evidently changed his mind about it more than once, and his announced plan for concluding it, as found in the letter to Sir Walter Raleigh, seems to present insuperable difficulties. Like the *Canterbury Tales*, it is only half finished, but we need not be disturbed about that. In the six books we have there is, as Dryden said of Chaucer, God's plenty. And the books are complete as they stand, each dealing with the quest of a single knight in which his peculiar virtue finds a field for action. Red Cross and Guyon go their separate ways in the first two books. Then, as if to provide variety, the next three books carry the same group of characters through a long series of actions. There are separate heroes assigned to the quests of these books, but all the main characters appear in all three books. The sixth book starts us on a new group of characters who were probably intended to provide continuing interest in a new succession of books, for although the hero achieves his quest there is much unfinished business among the minor characters. Almost as an afterthought the figure of Prince Arthur, a quite unhistorical Arthur, was added as the sum of all the virtues and assigned the task of rescuing such of the heroes as get into difficulties too great for their powers. Thus in Spenser's design were classic regularity and the single hero combined with the wandering profusion of medieval chivalric romance. Truly, Hobgoblin has run away with the garland of Apollo, but the garland is undamaged and Apollo did not refuse to look indulgently on the theft.

To the modern reader, particularly to one living in a monarchless democracy, the place of Queen Elizabeth in the poem and the compliments paid to her seem unduly great, but I think that they did not seem so to an Elizabethan Englishman. By him the sovereign was not regarded primarily as an individual but as the symbol of the nation. Praise of the prince was a form of patriotism and was quite as often a sincere expression of love of country as it was personal flattery. Too frequently our modern cynical attitude toward passages of this sort does not take that into account. Also we forget that Elizabeth was a truly great queen, one of the greatest rulers in English history. Of this her subjects were well aware, and they praised her with that unstinted exuberance so characteristic of the period. To believe that Spenser's attribution to her of the virtues celebrated in his poem was mercenary flattery is to misunderstand him entirely and to misunderstand the place which the queen occupies in it. Gloriana is the dispenser of true fame and glory in fairyland. But Elizabeth, we are told by the poet, is Gloriana. She is the earthly embodiment of the eternal idea for which Gloriana stands. It is for her to bestow glory upon those of her subjects who truly deserve it, and in so doing she shares her own glory with them.

With this general idea of the artistic form and ethical theme of the poem in mind, let us see what rewards the *Faerie Queene* has to offer us. At the outset let us frankly face the fact that modern readers do not know the poem, outside the first book or fragments of that book in anthologies. Therefore the story must be told before it can be discussed. If there is danger in summarizing briefly what a great poet has devoted many pages to, there is even greater danger in talking about something of which readers are entirely ignorant. The narrative core of the *Faerie Queene* is the group of continued stories in Books III, IV, and V, and I propose to break with tradition by discussing this portion first. We shall then return to Books I and II to examine Spenser's allegory, and finally we shall end with Book VI and the fragment of Book VII.

Britomart, the female knight, is the heroine of Book III, plays an important part in Book IV, and becomes the betrothed of Arthegal, the hero of Book V. She therefore forms the most important connecting link between these three books. Second to her in importance is Florimel, a timorous maiden who flies like a frightened fawn through all of Book III, meets her true love Marinel at the end of Book IV, and marries him in the third canto of Book V. Around these two main characters a number of minor knights and ladies appear and reappear from time to time. Chief of these are Arthegal, Scudamour, Satyrane, Marinel, and the boastful but cowardly Braggadochio among the men and Amoret, Belphoebe, and the false Florimel among the women. Arthur, of course, appears occasionally to rescue or assist the heroes.

In the beginning of Book III Arthur, Guyon, and Britomart, who is disguised as a man, are riding along when Florimel comes dashing past on a white palfrey, hotly pursued by a villainous forester. The two men, by no means immune to the charms of beauty in distress, fly off to rescue her, leaving Britomart to her own adventures. These are not slow in coming. Finding the Red Cross Knight attacked by six opponents outside a place called Castle Joyous, she helps him subdue them and they both enter the castle to spend the night. The nature of the proprietress is given away by her name, Malecasta, and we are not surprised to find her stealing into Britomart's bed, since the latter has refused to disarm and still passes for a man. Britomart and Red Cross leave the castle in disgust, ending the first canto. As her sex has been revealed by this incident, she finds it incumbent upon her to explain her martial career to her companion. It seems that she had seen her destined lover, Arthegal, in a magic mirror and heard a prediction from Merlin that her descendants will rule England. Being a maid who loves action, she has started out on a quest to find the man whose image has aroused her love. A magic spear, which overthrows all opponents, prevents her from coming to any harm. Leaving Red Cross after this recital, Britomart comes upon Marinel, a brave

youth who has ~~unfortunately~~ been brought up by his
mother to fear both love and women. Since he refuses her
passage across his land, she strikes him down and passes
on her way.

The story now returns to the pursuit of Florimel by the
two knights. Guyon soon drops out of the picture, but
Arthur finally comes across Florimel's dwarf, who tells
him the story of her love for Marinel, a love hitherto
fruitless because of his mother's training. In the meantime
Arthur's squire, Timias, has killed the wicked forester
but in turn has been ambushed and left for dead by the
latter's brothers. He is nursed back to life by Belphoebe,
with whom he falls desperately in love. The introduction
of Belphoebe into the story causes Spenser to put in one of
his apparent digressions, an elaborate description of the
Garden of Adonis, where Belphoebe and her twin sister
Amoret were brought up. Viewed in the larger scheme of
Spenser's whole poem and its interpretation, this description is too important to be called a digression, but it will
naturally appear as such on the first reading. Belphoebe,
after leaving the Garden of Adonis, had become a favorite
of Diana and was insensible to the power of love, whereas
Amoret, of whom we shall hear more later, was adopted by
Venus.

Florimel's adventures are next taken up. After many
dangers she reaches the sea and pushes off in a boat to
escape the beast who at that moment is pursuing her. In
the boat, unfortunately for her, is an old but lecherous
fisherman, and Florimel is saved only by the opportune
arrival of Proteus, who takes her as an honored guest to
his cave under the sea. He repeatedly makes love to her,
but she remains faithful to Marinel. While this is going
on, an old witch, whose son has fallen in love with Flori-

mel, complicates matters by fashioning a false Florimel out of snow. In spite of her icy nature this false Florimel is a great flirt and causes a lot of trouble in Book IV.

Cantos 9 and 10 deal with the case history of Hellenore, a young wife whose husband's miserliness and frigidity lead her to welcome seduction by Sir Paridel. When he deserts her, she becomes the common paramour of a flock of satyrs and seems to be enjoying the situation.

Book III ends with Britomart's rescue of the young bride, Amoret, from the castle of the enchanter Busirane, who had stolen her from her lover Scudamour on their wedding day. Busirane is torturing her inside the castle, while Scudamour, who has traced her thus far, is unable to force his way in through the curtain of fire which guards the entrance. Britomart is able to do this because the magic fire has no power against her chastity and complete purity of heart. This exploit, though introduced so late, must be considered her quest as heroine of the book, for her search after Arthegal is not completed until the middle of the fourth book.

Before continuing the story through the next two books let us pause for a moment to consider the significance of the narrative. In doing so we will be putting ourselves in the position of Spenser's readers in 1590, since only the first three books were published at that time. The third book is entitled the "Legend of Chastity" as a special compliment to Elizabeth, the Virgin Queen. That this title does not mean virginity alone is shown by the action itself and by Spenser's statement in the first canto that Britomart represents chaste affection, that is, true and honorable love. The heroine's first act is to fall in love, and her purpose thereafter is to find her lover, exchange vows with him, and, when it becomes necessary, rescue him from shameful captivity. Thus her adventures consist of incidents illustrative of the power of love. Her pure affection is contrasted with the lust of Malecasta, which Spenser unreservedly condemns, and the illicit outburst of Hellenore's natural instincts, for which Spenser provides a psychological excuse. The climax of the book is her generous undertaking of a hazardous rescue in order to reunite two faithful lovers. Britomart owes her enduring charm to the fact that she is chaste love *in action.* She is a dynamic force sweeping vigorously across the scene and spilling unceremoniously out of her way all those who, like Malecasta, are merely libidinous or who, like Marinel, are afraid of sexual love. On her very first appearance she delights us by bowling over Sir Guyon, the rather priggish hero of Temperance in Book II. Poor Guyon has just been through some very disturbing temptations of the flesh in rescuing a young knight from the clutches of a particularly luscious enchantress and is inclined to think that all love is evil. Spenser tells us that the palmer, who stands for Reason, and Arthur, the embodiment of all the virtues, soon reconciled the two and points the moral that there is no justification for a quarrel between "goodly temperance" and "affection chaste." In one way the passage is an anticipation of Milton's defense of the honest enjoyment of sexual intercourse in a marriage of true lovers. C. S. Lewis is right when he points out in his *Allegory of Love* that Spenser was the first great poet to treat love as an idealistic state of the emotions leading to marriage.

Britomart is not only contrasted with bad or deficient characters; she is also contrasted with two characters who may be called subsidiary heroines. These are Florimel and Belphoebe. Florimel, like Britomart, is already in love with her appointed mate; but, unlike Britomart, she is not a dynamic force. Instead she is the embodiment of female timidity. She is always seen flying from some man, and, like the heroines of the old movie serials, she never escapes one pursuer without falling into the clutches of another. Spenser emphasizes the fact that this behavior, along with her beauty, appeals to the protective and amorous instincts of every male in the story. Even Arthur is tempted to give up his pursuit of his unseen ideal, the fairy queen, and pursue Florimel instead. Belphoebe, on the other hand, has all the courage and martial success of Britomart but is completely lacking in the emotion of love. Her beauty is reserved and unapproachable. She has no objection to the devotion of Timias, and is even annoyed when she thinks he is guilty of transferring it to another lady, but she is quite incapable of returning it. In the introduction to the third book Spenser directly invites Elizabeth—who as queen demanded that her courtiers make love to her but could not, for political reasons, marry any of them—to see in Belphoebe an example of her chastity, as in Gloriana she was to see an example of her power and majesty. The parallel was perfect.

Britomart's major quest is the search for her lover Arthegal, a quest which is given a national as well as a personal importance by Merlin's prophecy that her descendants will rule England. This apparently seemed to Spenser too large a theme to be disposed of in a single book, so he provided a minor quest in the rescue of Amoret, a quest which specifically illustrates the power of chastity. This adventure provides several problems for the student of Spenser which are interesting enough to be mentioned here. The first problem is to answer the question: whose quest is the rescue of Amoret? As the story is told, it appears that Scudamour has pursued the enchanter Busirane to his castle but cannot penetrate the wall of flame which protects the gate. Britomart finds that the fire divides to let her pass, and she eventually conquers Busirane. The incident of the fire and Busirane's fear of a virgin knight make it clear that the quest can be performed only by the representative of chastity—Britomart. Yet in the letter to Sir Walter Raleigh we are told that Scudamour was at Gloriana's court when the news of Amoret's plight was brought in by a groom and that he, being her lover, then undertook the quest. This version of the origin of the quest is inconsistent with the narrative in the *Faerie Queene*, both here and in later passages in Book IV. It can best be explained either as a lapse of memory or as part of a new plan linking the stories more closely to Gloriana's court. The presence of a similar discrepancy in the letter to Raleigh in regard to the quest of Book II suggests the latter alternative. It also suggests that the letter is not an adequate guide to the poem as we have it.

The second problem is more difficult. What was to be the ultimate importance of Amoret and Scudamour in the weaving of the great tapestry of the *Faerie Queene?* And what was to be the occasion of their reunion? In all the editions of the poem since 1590 Scudamour, believing that Britomart has failed, finally leaves the castle of Busirane and begins a series of disconsolate wanderings which we occasionally witness in Books IV and V. But the first text of Book III, as it appeared in 1590, contained a different ending. The return of Britomart with the rescued Amoret finds Scudamour still stretched upon the ground in grief. At the sound of her voice he starts up:

> There did he see, that most on earth him joyd,
> His dearest love, the comfort of his dayes,
> Whose too long absence him had sore annoyd

And wearied his life with dull delayes:
Straight he upstarted from the loathed layes,
And to her ran with hasty egerness,
Like as a deare, that greedily embayes
In the coole soile, after long thirstinesse,
Which he in chace endured hath, now nigh breathlesse.

Lightly he clipt her twixt his armes twaine,
And streightly did embrace her body bright,
Her body, late the prison of sad paine,
Now the sweet lodge of love and deare delight:
But she faire lady overcommen quight
Of huge affection, did in pleasure melt,
And in sweet ravishment pourd out her spright:
No word they spake, nor earthly thing they felt,
But like two senceless stocks in long embracement dwelt.

This passage shows that Spenser's original intention was to reunite the lovers immediately, after which they doubtless would have disappeared from the rest of the story. When he set about continuing the poem, he realized that such a definite stop at the end of Book III might seem too conclusive, especially as he intended to continue all the other plots started in that book. The puzzling thing is that these are all concluded by the end of Book V, but Amoret and Scudamour still seek sorrowfully for each other over the unmapped ways of fairyland.

The third problem is to determine whether there is any allegorical meaning in the separation of Scudamour and Amoret and the torture of the latter by a vile enchanter. This involves a consideration of the general method of allegory in Book III and of the previous history of the two lovers. The allegory of love in this book is presented by a series of contrasted case histories rather than built up as a progressive argument. Examples of different situations in love are given, many minor ones being added to those mentioned in our brief summary. Different degrees of unchaste love are exemplified, on the one hand, and different situations in chaste love, on the other. Britomart, Florimel, and Amoret are all chaste lovers, but their fortunes differ as do their characters. Only Britomart lives a full and satisfactory life in which all her powers are utilized as well as disciplined. If this be true, what then is the interpretation of Britomart's rescue of Amoret? Amoret, imprisoned and tortured by Busirane, is a martyr to her faithful love for Scudamour. Why is she a martyr? Is it only for the sake of the plot, to provide a sympathetic character for Britomart to rescue, or is there some reason in her own character? To settle this question, we need to examine Spenser's account of her birth and upbringing.

Belphoebe and Amoret, although described as twins conceived in spotless purity by parthenogenesis, must certainly represent opposites. Belphoebe, adopted by Diana, is too cold and lacks the power to love. Amoret, adopted by Venus, should therefore be characterized by an excess of love and a corresponding lack of cool restraint; but, since she is called by Spenser an example of true love and the lodestar of chaste affection, it is obvious that this excess cannot extend to any unchaste actions. It is perhaps significant that we are told rather pointedly that she was brought up as the companion of Cupid's daughter, Pleasure. There is no harm in this, but it fits in with the whole picture of Amoret's background. Under the tutelage of Venus she has grown up without spiritual discipline. Her inborn purity keeps her perfectly loyal to her chosen lover, but the weakness of her character puts her at the mercy of Busirane. She cannot resist capture by the forces of the lustful magician; she can only suffer gallantly under his torture and refuse to surrender her will. That Scudamour, who bears the image of Cupid on his shield, shares the same weakness is shown by his inability to rescue her. Spenser was well aware that the innocent suffer in this world, and he was always interested in looking for the reasons.

The rescue of Amoret can now be seen in its real importance. In spite of its late introduction into the narrative of Book III it is not just another adventure, thrown in to bring the book to a dramatic close. In her other adventures Britomart has merely been contrasted with vice or timidity. Here she appears in her full capacity as chaste love in action. Only a knight whose heart was disciplined in chastity was able to enter the castle and survive its dangers unharmed, but it is equally true that only one with a heart full of generous love would have undertaken to pass through those perilous flames for the sake of another's sufferings. Britomart is not, like Red Cross, saving her own soul nor has she, like Guyon, a guide and mentor at hand to keep her from spiritual danger; she is not even engaged in a solemnly accepted mission. She comes across human need and suffering quite by chance, and on the instant her overflowing love offers itself without reserve in service.

> I will with proofe of last extremity
> Deliver her from thence, or with her for you die

she says to Scudamour. It is this lively spontaneity which makes her so attractive. That she has always been the most popular of Spenser's characters is a tribute to his triumphant solution of that most difficult of all the problems of fiction, the problem of how to make a thoroughly good character interesting.

Book IV is the most confusing book in the *Faerie Queene*. Not only do the knights announced as the prototypes of friendship, the virtue assigned to this book, fail to perform any significant action, but it is also unfortunately true that Britomart and Florimel continue to steal the show and leave the new characters in the background. The book has no unity of plot, and it alone of all the books in the poem contains no quest to be performed. Nevertheless, it has an important function in binding together the third and fifth books. The treatment of the theme of friendship, such as it is, follows the episodic method of Book III. A number of incidents occur which illustrate true friendship, on the one hand, and false or pretended friendship, on the other. Unfortunately none of these incidents is memorable. What one retains out of the rather confusing experience of reading Book IV is all related to love, not friendship: Britomart's discovery of her destined lover, Belphoebe's strange jealousy at finding Timias tenderly caring for the wounded Amoret, and the dismay of the knights infatuated by the false Florimel when she deserts them for the cowardly Braggadochio. The action begins by the introduction of Ate (Discord) as the opposite of true friendship. With her are characters already introduced in Book III, Blandamour and Paridell. They are joined first by Scudamour, who is persuaded by Ate's slander that Amoret has been unfaithful to him, and later by the false Florimel whom the witch had made out of snow. She immediately exposes the shallowness of the professed friendship of the two knights by causing a quarrel between them. Eventually the party arrives at a pavilion where Satyrane is about to hold a tournament to determine who shall possess the famous girdle of the true Florimel, which she had dropped on the shore when escaping into the fisherman's boat. Tournaments were not Spenser's strong point—he lacked Malory's hearty enjoyment of broken spears and bones—but in this case he at least worked hard to provide variety.

The jolly Satyrane, who is secretly the favorite knight of most readers, overthrows all comers until a "salvage knight"—that darling of medieval romance—arrives to topple him down in his turn. This strange knight's triumph is short-lived, for Britomart, still disguised as a man, comes dashing in at the last minute with her magic spear to upset everything and win the prize.

The ladies' part in the program now begins, for the most beautiful lady was to receive the girdle, and she in turn was to be awarded to the knight who won the tournament. This beauty contest is one of Spenser's rare ironical passages. In spite of all the genuine beauties presented to view, it is the false Florimel who receives the most acclaim; yet when she tries on the girdle, which we have been told is symbolic of chastity, it refuses to stay on her:

irony

> Then many other ladies likewise tried
> About their tender loins to knit the same;
> But it would not on none of them abide,
> But when they thought it fast, eftsoones it was untied.
>
> Which when that scornful Squire of Dames did view,
> He loudly gan to laugh and thus to jest:
> Alas for pity that so fair a crew,
> As like cannot be seen from east to west,
> Cannot find one this girdle to invest,
> Fie on the man that did it first invent,
> To shame us all with this, *Ungirt unblest.*
> Let never lady to his love assent
> That hath this day so many so unmanly shent.

The laughter of the cynical squire, in which all the other knights join heartily in spite of their ladies' disapproval, is not the end of this satirical scene. False Florimel, having been adjudged the most beautiful is awarded to the disguised Britomart. She refuses the award by saying that

Amoret, who has been with her since the end of Book III, is her ladylove. Ate then stirs up all the knights to quarrel over the disposal of the prize until finally Satyrane settles the matter by leaving the choice to the lady herself. The disturbance ceases, and each knight gazes wishfully on the false flirt. She, says Spenser, looks long upon each one as though she wishes to please them all, and then chooses—the cowardly boaster, Braggadochio! Thus at one stroke the knights are paid off for having admired false rather than true beauty, and the false beauty herself, who is all the time not a real woman at all but a snow image made by a witch, receives a fitting mate in the very model of unknightly conduct.

The next scene gives us one of the plot climaxes of the *Faerie Queene*, Britomart's discovery of Arthegal. The salvage knight at the tournament had been Arthegal in disguise. Angered at his discomfiture by Britomart, he is waiting for a chance to encounter her again when he meets Scudamour. The latter also is enraged against Britomart because he thinks that she (whom he and Arthegal believe to be a man) has stolen Amoret from him. No sooner have they learned that each is seeking her than she herself appears. Striking down Scudamour with a single blow of her lance, she turns her attention to Arthegal. Although unhorsed at the first encounter, he recovers himself and soon injures Britomart's horse so severely that she in turn dismounts. Finally Arthegal hacks her helmet apart, revealing her face and her golden hair. Stupefied at this discovery, he is soon overwhelmed with admiration and love. Britomart now recognizes him as the hero seen in her vision, and a mutual plighting of faith takes place. The revelation of Britomart's sex having removed all of Scudamour's unfounded anger, he inquires of her what she has done with Amoret. Britomart replies that while she was sleeping one day her fair charge disappeared and could not be found again.

The continuation of Amoret's story brings us to the third memorable scene in Book IV. We must remember that Timias, Arthur's squire, had fallen in love with Amoret's sister Belphoebe and is following her with dog-like devotion in spite of her disdain of such feelings. Now Amoret, upon leaving Britomart for a short walk in the woods, fell into the clutches of a wild man of monstrous appearance. Timias turns up just in time to engage her captor in combat. The latter, however, is getting rather the better of it when Belphoebe joins the fray and finally kills him with an arrow as he flees from her. While this is going on, Timias is giving tender attention to the unconscious girl. Belphoebe, returning, witnesses his caresses and finds that she is capable of jealousy even if not of love:

> Which when she saw, with sudden glancing eye,
> Her noble heart with sight thereof was filled
> With deep disdain and great indignity,
> That in her wrath she thought them both have thrilled
> With that selfe arrow which the carle had killed:
> Yet held her wrathful hand from vengeance sore,
> But drawing nigh ere he her well beheld;
> "Is this the faith?" she said, and said no more,
> But turned her face, and fled away for evermore.

This humanizing of the icily aloof Belphoebe is one of the most satisfying things in the whole poem.

The rest of the fourth book is miscellaneous. Arthur takes charge of Amoret but does not succeed in restoring her to Scudamour. The last two cantos bring us back to the story of Florimel, who has been imprisoned by Proteus because she will not accept his love. Marinel, whom she loves, attends a great feast given by Proteus to celebrate the marriage of the Thames and Medway rivers. Passing beneath her prison window, he hears her bewailing her fate and telling of her love for him. This leads Marinel to entreat his mother, a sea nymph, to effect the rescue of Florimel by appealing to Neptune. The appeal is successful, and at last we witness the end of Florimel's long flight from pursuing males. The objections of Marinel's mother are overridden, and the pair are happily married early in the fifth book.

It is now time to return to the question raised at the beginning of this account of Book IV: why is the virtue of friendship not made central to the plot instead of being left to minor incidents? The answer lies partly in the history of the composition of the poem and partly in Spenser's conception of the relation between the three virtues of love, friendship, and justice.

In a recent book on the evolution of the *Faerie Queene*, Mrs. Josephine W. Bennett has made it clear that Spenser did not write the poem in the order in which it now stands and that the idea of arranging it according to the virtues was a later imposition upon much of the earlier narrative. The poet obviously had on hand material relating to the continued stories of Britomart and Florimel which he wished to use in order to keep those stories moving toward their conclusions in Book V. On the other hand, his final scheme, which named this the book of friendship, made it necessary for him to introduce new material which would illustrate that virtue. This set a problem in construction which certainly was not successfully solved. We can easily observe the attempts which Spenser made to introduce the theme of friendship into the narrative. First of all, we must note that the heading of the book, whether supplied by the publisher in ignorance or by Spenser in haste, is quite inaccurate. Cambel and Triamond (wrongly given as Telamond in the heading) are neither the best examples of friendship nor the principal characters. They represent Spenser's attempt to continue Chaucer's "Squire's Tale" and are played up strongly in the second and third cantos. After this, one expects to find them dominating the action, but they appear again only in the tournament in the fourth canto, which, by the way, they do not win. Their friendship is stressed, it is true, but they do not perform any important action illustrating that virtue, and they have no place in the plot.

The most consistent attempt to develop the theme of the book occurs in Cantos 7, 8, and 9, where it is linked with the important figure of Arthur. When Belphoebe, by killing the lustful wild man, rescued Amoret, she also rescued a girl named Aemylia who had been a captive of the same man. Aemylia's lover, a young squire named Amyas, and his friend Placidas provide the best illustration of the titular virtue. Placidas voluntarily accepts imprisonment in order to help his friend. Escaping later on, he is pursued by his giant captor, Corflambo, who is about to kill him when Arthur arrives. Arthur kills the giant, forces an entry into the castle, and reunites the friends. While the whole party is recuperating, he tactfully straightens out their love affairs. Here we have, as Mrs. Bennett has pointed out, a miniature book of friendship, which is given further prominence by its association with the figure of Arthur. In the first and second books Arthur had performed a rescue of the hero in the eighth canto; consequently, by analogy, we should regard Placidas and not Triamond as the hero of the fourth book.

Another, though less striking, attempt to illustrate the operation of friendship is found in Britomart's relation to

Amoret in the first half of Book IV. This one at least has the merit of being attached to the main plot. We must remember that Amoret, when first rescued by Britomart, mistakes her for a man. This causes her to be very fearful of her rescuer until a situation arises in a castle they are visiting which causes Britomart to reveal her sex. From that time on their intimacy grows until in Canto 6 (stanza 46) we are told that Britomart's relation to Amoret expresses the power of faithful friendship just as her relation to Arthegal expresses the power of true love, both being grounded in virtue. Consequently we may say that Book IV illustrates friendship between members of the female sex as well as the male. It is possible that the incident of Timias and Amoret is meant to suggest the dangers that may lie in attempts at friendship, rather than love, between members of opposite sexes.

The realization that Britomart in Book IV illustrates both love and friendship brings us to the consideration of the connection between these two virtues and justice, the virtue exemplified by Arthegal in Book V. Spenser's use of one continuous plot, centered in Britomart and Arthegal, for the three books shows clearly enough his desire to make us think about the connections between them. Actually, all these virtues are included in the Christian conception of love itself, and the three linked books portray the three manifestations of love: love between man and woman (sexual love), love between man and man or woman and woman (friendship), and love in the whole human community (justice). Britomart is a type of the first and second (perhaps even of the third, as we shall see in Book V), Arthegal of the first and third; there is no major character who typifies the second and third together. Had there been a real hero for Book IV, he might have exemplified this combination. From the logical and ethical point of view this lack is doubtless serious. Friendship is necessary to true and lasting love between man and woman and is also fundamental to justice in society. The ideal of justice is that each citizen shall receive such treatment as one would give one's friend or, as the Bible says, one's self. However this may be, Spenser was not simply writing moral allegory; he was creating characters and telling a story. The story of these three books is primarily the story of Britomart's love for Arthegal and secondarily Florimel's love for Marinel. Evidently he did not wish a third pair— or even a third individual—to share this interest.

If in Book IV narrative is stressed at the expense of allegory, in Book V it is the latter which triumphs over narrative. Unfortunately it is allegory of a very wooden and unconvincing type in most places. Whereas in Book III the situations were of real interest as typical examples of love as we know it, in Book V not only do most of the examples of justice seem forced and unnatural but they seem to happen to a number of extremely uninteresting people. The parts of the book which have to do with the continued plot of these three books are told with undiminished vigor, but the incidents illustrating Arthegal's career as champion of justice rather than as the lover of Britomart are uninspired and give the impression of having been ground out by a flagging invention under the necessity of finishing a task.

Whether this was actually so, we have no means of knowing. It is easy enough to show, however, that portions of it were written in a depressed and pessimistic mood. The prologue states with some bitterness that not only

men but even nature's works have sadly degenerated
since the beginning:

> For that which all men then did vertue call
> Is now called vice; and that which vice was hight
> Is now hight vertue, and so us'd of all:
> Right now is wrong, and wrong that was, is right,
> As all things else in time are changed quight.
> Ne wonder, for the heaven's revolution
> Is wandred far from where it first was pight,
> And so do make contrarie constitution
> Of all this lower world, toward his dissolution.

And this is followed up with some very interesting astronomical proof. Again, in the concluding cantos, where one
might expect an expression of faith in the power of justice,
Spenser falters where he firmly trod. The incident of
Burbon, with his discarded shield of faith and his unwilling
lady, was obviously meant to leave a bad taste in the
mouth; and the last we see of Arthegal is a man recalled
from his quest with his work only half done and his fame
already under attack by envy and detraction. Nothing
could illustrate better than these two passages the danger
of introducing contemporary history into an epic. The
scheme of the *Faerie Queene* called for a series of books in
which each individual hero must successfully achieve a
quest. In the first three books this is done wholeheartedly;
the forces opposing the hero are completely routed. In the
fourth book, where there is no single hero, all the forces of
evil have been overcome and the book ends with a happy
solution to the love problem of Florimel and Marinel. In
Book V the quest of Arthegal is the rescue of Irena (Ireland) from Grantorto (Spain and the Roman church). As
a freely imagined character in an allegorical narrative he
should not only rescue the lady, which he does, but also
remain a glorious and triumphant figure to the end. Had

[93]

Arthegal remained a mythical ancestor of British kings (his function in Books III and IV) purveying justice to the Ireland of Arthurian legend, he would undoubtedly have enjoyed the type of grand finale accorded to the Red Cross Knight in Book I, to whose career his own is somewhat similar. Unfortunately Spenser decided to take the concluding incidents of his story from contemporary history in the Low Countries, France, and Ireland. In these countries the Protestant cause, although in most respects holding its own, was not markedly triumphant in the 1590's. The unsatisfactory ending of the Irena affair probably represents the recall of Lord Grey in 1582, but the failure of Arthegal to establish permanent justice typifies the consistent failure of Elizabeth's halfhearted Irish policy throughout Spenser's life. This is the only place in the whole poem where the representation of contemporary events exercises a controlling influence on the plot. The result is an artistic failure. Arthegal has not really completed his quest.

The narrative of Book V breaks into three parts: the marriage of Florimel and Marinel, the continuation of the Britomart and Arthegal love story, and the deeds of Arthegal exemplifying justice. The marriage and its accompanying tournament were reserved for Book V in order to strengthen the linking-up of plot structure throughout the three books we have been discussing. Here for the last time we see gathered together most of the company of knights and ladies with whom we are familiar. The festivities are linked to the theme of justice by the fact that Arthegal wins the tournament and by two pieces of enforced restitution. Braggadochio is made to restore Guyon's horse, which he had stolen in Book II; and Florimel's girdle, which the false Florimel has been carrying around even though it does not fit her, is given back to its rightful owner. This latter event is part of a highly dramatic scene done in Spenser's best style. Since Arthegal had borrowed Braggadochio's shield for disguise, Braggadochio is pub- licly congratulated by the bride, in whose honor the tour- nament was held. With characteristic boorishness he re- jects her thanks and announces that his own lady, the false Florimel, excels her and all others in beauty. At this rude shock poor Florimel leaves the hall in dismay:

> Then forth he brought his snowy Florimele,
> Whom Trompart had in keeping there beside,
> Covered from people's gazement with a vele;
> Whom when discovered they had throughly eyed,
> With great amazement they were stupefied,
> And said that surely Florimell it was,
> Or if it were not Florimell so tried,
> That Florimell herselfe she then did pas.
> So feeble skill of perfect things the vulgar has.

> Which whenas Marinell beheld likewise,
> He was therewith exceedingly dismayd;
> Ne wist he what to thinke, or to devise,
> But like as one whom feends have made affrayd,
> He long astonisht stood, ne ought he sayd,
> Ne ought he did, but with fast fixed eyes
> He gazed still upon that snowy mayd;
> Whom ever as he did the more avize,
> The more to be true Florimell he did surmize.

Arthegal breaks in upon the bridegroom's dilemma by proving that Braggadochio was not the real winner of the tournament. If he is a false knight, Arthegal continues, doubtless the lady is a false lady too:

> This lady which he showeth here
> Is not, I wager, Florimell at all,
> But some fayre franion, fit for such a fere,
> That by misfortune in his hand did fall.
> For proofe whereof he bade them Florimell forth call.

So forth the noble ladie was ybrought,
Adorn'd with honor and all comely grace:
Whereto her bashfull shamefastness ywrought
A great increase in her fayre blushing face,
As roses did with lillies interlace.
For of those words, the which that boaster threw,
She inly yet conceived great disgrace.
Whom whenas all the people such did view,
They shouted loud, and signes of gladnesse all did shew.

Then did he set her by that snowy one,
Like the true saint by the image set,
Of both their beauties to make paragone,
And triall, whether should the honor get.
Straightway so soone as both together met,
Th'enchaunted damzell vanisht into nought:
Her snowy substance melted as with heat,
Ne of that goodly hue remained ought
But th'emptie girdle which about her waste was wrought.

This recalls the scene in Book IV where the false Florimel did win the beauty contest, the true Florimel being absent. It is part of the vigor of Spenser's character creation that he makes his false beauty blind men's eyes and carry away the admiration of everyone until faced with the original. We should also notice the characteristic behavior of Florimel. Timorous throughout the poem, she shrinks away from Braggadochio's insults. Britomart would have behaved quite differently.

In fact, Britomart does behave quite differently not long after this. Florimel's wedding occurs in Canto 3; in Cantos 4–6 we have the story of Arthegal's strange submission to the monstrous regiment of women in the person of Radegund and his rescue by Britomart. This is one of the most striking pieces of narrative in the *Faerie Queene* and merits close attention. Arthegal, after some rather dull exploits in the opening cantos, returns to the stage in

Canto 4. Here he meets a knight named Turpine being led ignominiously off to execution by a group of women. Finding that they are followers of Radegund, who has set up a sort of Amazonian state under her dictatorship, he proceeds to her town and challenges her to combat in order to avenge the male sex. Radegund, furious at the rescue of her prisoner, puts up a strong fight but is finally knocked senseless by Arthegal. As he is unlacing her helmet in order to cut off her head, he is overwhelmed by the beauty of her face, even though it was, as Spenser says, bathed in blood and sweat. Struck with compassion at the thought of having hurt such a fair creature, he throws away his sword and refuses to fight any longer. Radegund comes out of her swoon and promptly captures him. The result of this ill-advised softness is doubly disastrous. Not only is Arthegal sentenced to hard labor and the wearing of women's clothing, but the unfortunate Turpine, whom he had set out to save, is executed after all. To make his position worse, Radegund falls in love with him and has no intention of ever releasing him unless he will return her love. In the meantime Talus, Arthegal's groom, makes his way back to Britomart, who has been suffering the pangs of jealousy at her lover's failure to return from his mission. The scene of her interview with Talus is too long to quote. Suffice it to say that her eager questioning extracts the answer that Arthegal is vanquished and lies in wretched bondage. She is full of sympathy and concern until she learns that his conqueror is a woman. "The rest myself too readily can spell," she cries and retires to her room in angry tears. Made to understand at last what has really happened, she transfers her rage to Radegund, throws on her armor, and sets out to wreak vengeance on the woman who would take her lord away from her.

Edmund Spenser and the Faerie Queene

On her way to this rescue Britomart has a narrow escape from treachery one night at the hands of Dolon, who thinks she is Arthegal because Talus is with her. The next day she overthrows Dolon's sons at the Perilous Bridge and proceeds to the Temple of Isis, where she spends the next night. Here she has a remarkable vision concerning a crocodile, interpreted by the priests of Isis as a prophecy of her union with Arthegal. This visit to the temple is symbolic, since Osiris, husband of Isis in Egyptian mythology, was the god of justice and his symbol is said by the priests to be the crocodile. But Isis herself was "that part of justice which is equity." In this way Britomart, as the prospective wife of Arthegal, is made to appear as a champion of justice also. At the moment, indeed, justice is badly in need of a champion to rescue her own knight from his self-imposed defeat and imprisonment. Britomart therefore hastens on to challenge Radegund to single combat. She is wounded in the ensuing fight but rallies her strength to fell her opponent with a mighty stroke. Unlike Arthegal, instead of waiting for Radegund to come to herself again, she cuts off head and helmet both with one blow. With only a brief reproach to her unfortunate lover that the force of strength and courage is nought when the mind can be seduced, she has him reclothed in manly raiment and establishes him as king of the city, thus reversing the female rule of his predecessor. Spenser makes a strong point of this and emphasizes the fact that Britomart did not take the government of the country upon herself but gave it to a man.

With this act of love and self-restraint Britomart passes out of the *Faerie Queene*. Almost certainly she would have appeared again if Spenser had finished the poem; one can hardly doubt that he was planning one of his most splendid pageants for her wedding to Arthegal. Even as it is, she remains the most human and the most memorable person among his knights and ladies. Her warmth of emotion, her generosity to others, her dynamic conception of chastity, even her fits of jealousy, make her a really living and lovable figure. To those who object that she is not feminine because she wears heavy armor and knocks down several male knights in rather boisterous fashion I recommend the dainty Florimel, who I am sure carried a scented lace handkerchief. There is food for all tastes in the *Faerie Queene*.

In Canto 8 Arthegal, who now resumes his long-delayed rescue of Irena, meets Prince Arthur in the act of saving a maiden named Samient from two paynim knights, followers of the Soldan. From her they learn of the great enmity between this soldan and her mistress, the maiden queen Mercilla. The two knights immediately undertake the overthrow of this tyrant, and after his death they ride to Mercilla's court. Now Mercilla is obviously Elizabeth in her capacity of merciful judge, and we find her surrounded by three virgins whose names signify justice, law, and peace. When Arthur and Arthegal arrive, Mercilla receives them with great dignity. Since she is at that moment engaged in the trial of Duessa (whom all readers of Book I will remember to stand for Mary of Scotland), she invites her distinguished guests to sit beside her and hear the evidence. Duessa is accused of conspiring against the person and throne of Mercilla and of being an enemy of true morality and religion, but Pity, Nobility, Regard of Womanhood, and other special pleaders make such an appeal on her behalf that Arthur "woxe much enclined to her part through sad terror of so dreadful fate." Seeing this, the prosecuting attorney, Zeal, calls to the stand Murder,

Sedition, Adultery, and Impiety. Arthegal, on the other hand, has been cured of sentimental sympathy by his experience with Radegund and sets his mind with constant firmness against all interference with strict justice. All finally condemn Duessa, and she is executed, even though Mercilla's compassion delays the carrying-out of the sentence for some time.

The Belge, Burbon, and Irena episodes, which occupy the last three cantos, are less interesting than this one. The inconclusiveness and pessimism of the last two have already been pointed out. The trial of Duessa is actually the high point of the allegory of justice. Duessa's crimes were notorious and are familiar to all readers who have gone through the poem up to this point. They now see a dangerous enemy of right and truth brought to the bar and tried with all the dignity and impartiality which should characterize what Spenser calls the most sacred of all virtues. Duessa is allowed her defense and even wins the sympathy of many people, yet she is inexorably given the reward of her past deeds. Here Spenser used contemporary history to better effect than in the cantos which follow. The event of Mary's trial and execution was one of the great decisive actions of Elizabeth's reign, as compared with the continuing problems of war in France and the Low Countries and the ever recurring uprisings in Ireland, and it illustrated the triumph of justice. The only criticism one can make is that it has nothing to do with Arthegal. By tying his hero up with a contemporary general, whether Grey, Norris, or both of them, Spenser lost the power to proceed with a free hand in making the plot carry out the meaning of the allegory. The extent of his failure may be seen by comparing the action of this book with the similar allegorical action of Book I, where every event simultaneously carries on the story of the hero and the importance of holiness in the life of man.

We may well question, too, whether Arthegal is a satisfactory hero for Book V. In the first place he is a relatively inactive hero. Spenser saw fit to give him as a groom the iron man, Talus, with his irresistible flail. Since Talus, because of his metal construction (which to modern readers is unfortunately reminiscent of their childhood friend, the Tin Woodman of Oz), cannot suffer wounds, he rides roughshod over all the opponents of Arthegal. So convenient is this method of disposing of troublesome enemies, particularly if they are too numerous for comfort, that we find Arthegal relying more and more on his invincible groom and less and less on his own strong right arm. Here allegory and narrative again are not well adjusted. Spenser wished to show that theoretical justice requires the aid of an efficient police force if it is to make its decisions operative, but he has carried the illustration of this point so far that it destroys the appeal of his hero as a brave man. It is noteworthy by contrast that Britomart scorns the assistance of Talus in the affair at the Perilous Bridge. The objection that Arthegal is too unstable temperamentally for the prototype of justice may be hypercritical, but some evidence exists to support it. At the end of the argument with Braggadochio about Guyon's stolen horse Arthegal becomes so furious that he is about to kill the false boaster on the spot until he is pacified by Guyon himself. And his completely irrational submission to Radegund sacrifices the life of the man he was trying to save and would have sacrificed Irena too if Britomart had not come to the rescue. Such a fatal weakness for female beauty may be human enough, but it seems out of place in one who is symbolizing justice. Now it may be that the answer to this criticism is that Arthegal, like the Red Cross Knight in Book I, represents a man striving to achieve the titular virtue rather than a man already completely possessing it. If so, we miss in Book V the arduous process of rehabilitation by which the hero of Book I reaches his goal. We might also say that Guyon's attendant palmer (Reason) would have been a better companion for Arthegal than the robot Talus. Finally, we return to the point already made that Arthegal is not shown carrying out successfully any great triumph of justice.

To the Elizabethans the spice of contemporary reference was enough. The last five cantos contain in allegorical form a commentary on the history of England in the decade preceding 1595. This decade had seen England forced out of the cautious neutrality favored by Burghley and into open war with Spain and with the Catholic party in France. The patriotic war party, led in earlier days by the earl of Leicester and now led by the earl of Essex, had come into their own at last, and Spenser rejoiced with them. The first step had been armed intervention in the Netherlands in support of the Dutch rebels in 1585. Then had come the defeat of the Grand Armada in 1588 and the expedition to aid Henry IV of France in 1590–93. Indecisive as some of these actions were—the campaign in Brittany was a failure —they constituted a complete change of policy. What Book V celebrates in the execution of Duessa, the rescue of Samient and Belge, and the incident of Sir Burbon is the decision to cease temporizing and fight openly for the Protestant cause. When Spenser thinks of justice in this second half of the book, it is international justice he is thinking of, and what inspires him is the sight of England taking at last the place in international affairs which he had always hoped she would take.

The Narrative Poet

It would be possible, if one wished, to consider the continued block of narrative in Books III, IV, and V as a separate poem. As such it could claim in its own right a high place in its class. Its bulk, somewhere around fifteen thousand lines, is much greater than that of *Paradise Lost*, and much more of it is good reading. Starting out as an imitation of the episodic method of Ariosto—we know this from Harvey's comment in 1580—it was strengthened by the imposition upon it of the controlling theme of the threefold allegory of love. This control is not evenly exercised nor does it always produce results of the highest order, but for better or worse it gives the work a depth and significance which the gay pageant of *Orlando Furioso* lacks. In Britomart, Florimel, Belphoebe, and Amoret it provides a colorful and highly interesting variety of heroines whose traits are played off against each other very effectively. If the men seem not quite so good, it is only because the women set an extremely high standard. Arthegal, with all his faults, is a striking personality and the genial Satyrane an unusually likable one. Braggadochio is handled with great skill to serve both as a comic character and as a controlling figure in what may be called the antiplot, that is, the activities of a group of false knights and ladies who serve as a contrast to the noble characters. If Spenser had never written more of the *Faerie Queene* than these three books, he would not be so great a poet as he is, but he would still take very high rank.

CHAPTER V

THE ALLEGORIST
(*Faerie Queene*, I – II)

THE central books of the *Faerie Queene*, Books III–V, differ markedly from the remaining books in the fact that they are linked together by a continuous plot. Books I and II, which precede them, have nothing in common but the figure of Arthur. It is true that the Red Cross Knight and Sir Guyon, the heroes of these two books, appear as occasional figures in the three central books, but they have nothing to do with the plot. In Book VI there are no carryover characters from the rest of the poem except Arthur, who performs his usual rescue in Canto 8. The central books are also different in the relation of plot to allegory. In them we have reason to suspect that an allegorical framework·has been superimposed upon a story originally composed from a different point of view with new incidents then added to build up the new purpose. In Books I and II, on the other hand, it is apparent that the story was from the first meant to carry the weight of allegorical meaning. Book VI continues the type of narrative found in its immediate predecessors but starts fresh with an entirely new set of characters. I shall therefore leave it for later consideration and devote the present chapter to a discussion of the first two books.

At first sight Books I and II present certain striking similarities. In each there is a definite quest for the hero, a quest which requires of the performer certain moral and religious qualities. In each the hero, who has been separated from his moral guide, suffers an exhausting experience, after which he is rescued by Arthur and taken to a house of instruction in virtue. In each the author uses openly allegorical names most of the time and keeps his moral purpose in the center of our attention. There are, however, some very important differences. Most noticeable to the casual reader is the lack of a heroine in Book II, a lack which is psychologically important in certain places. Also of importance for its effect upon the reader is the fact that Guyon always wins; his rescue by Arthur is necessary not because Guyon has been overcome by an enemy but because his resistance to the temptations of Mammon have so exhausted his energy that he has fallen into a deep sleep and is at the mercy of new enemies of whom he is unaware. It is true that his unfailing success is often due to the presence of his accompanying palmer, who symbolizes Reason, rather than to his own unaided merit, but there is nevertheless in Guyon a certain smugness which the Red Cross Knight avoids by his very human capacity for getting into trouble. Finally, the plot of Book II is much more episodic and less easily remembered than that of Book I. From Book II one recalls certain scenes and characters; from Book I one retains a vivid consciousness of an organic, developing story.

Book I, like Book VI, is remarkable for its independence of the rest of the *Faerie Queene*. Both of them are linked to the rest of the poem only by the figure of Arthur. It is true that Duessa, Archimago, Satyrane, and the Red Cross Knight all appear occasionally in Books II–V, but they never seriously affect the action of these books. The subtraction of Book I would not make anything in the rest of the poem less clear or understandable. In its strictly religious allegory it is set apart from the rest and may once have been intended as a separate piece of work. It can hardly have been that early fragment which Harvey saw and objected to in 1580. However that may be, as we have it now, it has been excellently adapted to its place as the opening section of the poem. It gives a magnificent picture of Arthur, who is to link all the books and be the successful suitor of Gloriana; it deals with the champion of England, St. George; and it presents Queen Elizabeth, in the character of Una, as the triumphant symbol of Protestant faith.

The story of the Red Cross Knight and Una is unique in the *Faerie Queene* in the care evidently bestowed upon it. Its plot is dramatic and highly unified. Every detail of both narrative and allegory is fitted to its function with precision, and the decorations, which in the other books often seem structurally out of proportion, are all beautifully integrated with the action. This beauty of design doubtless owes a good deal to the revision given the book when it was selected to open the poem, but it is mainly the result of a clear allegorical purpose from the beginning. The characters and incidents have all been chosen for the specific purpose of enacting the drama of man's spiritual life. The elements of this drama were traditional in the church and in religious literature. Being a child of God, man seeks holiness; being an imperfect or fallen creature, he inevitably becomes a captive to sin. The grace of God, an outpouring of the divine love, raises him up again so that he is able to conquer the forces of evil and gain eternal blessedness. This sequence of human fate was known to every literate person in Spenser's day. His task was to find an artistically satisfying fiction with which to express it. For his hero he turned to the field of chivalric romance, but his hero's adventures, though told in a chivalric

setting, are those of Mankind or Everyman in the moral
plays. The hero is called St. George, and in the end he at-
tains sainthood, but before the final victory he is made to
suffer humiliation for his sins. It is in his rescue from this
humiliation that Spenser's early preoccupation with the
Revelation of St. John appears in the killing of the seven-
headed beast of Duessa by Arthur, who here performs the
function of the Savior in the Revelation. This combination
of medieval romance, saint's life, and the Bible is fused together by the poet's imagination into a single satisfying
story, every part of which is not only dramatic in itself but
also contributory to a grand conclusion in which the hero's
winning of his lady perfectly coincides with the religious
significance of the theme.

With this idea of the central allegory in our minds we
are in a position to consider the narrative. Canto 1 starts
off at a fast clip. Una and her knight, accompanied by a
dwarf, are riding along in pursuit of the quest assigned by
Gloriana when a sudden shower sends them into the woods
for shelter. Here the knight meets and overcomes the
dragon Error. This victory is ironical, for he is soon to
succumb to other forms of error through the deceit of his
enemies. The first of these enemies is the magician Archimago, who appears in the form of a holy hermit offering
lodging for the night. As soon as the hero and heroine are
safely asleep, Archimago pulls out his magic books, calls
up two spirits to aid him, and gets to work. After polluting
the knight's mind with amorous dreams, he sends one of
the spirits, in counterfeit likeness of Una, to the knight's
bed, saying that love of him has kept her sleepless. This
attempt fails, because Red Cross's first reaction is to be
deeply shocked; he sends the false Una back again with
polite evasions of her obvious intent. Archimago is now

forced to produce stronger evidence of Una's unworthiness. Dressing the other spirit as a young squire, he puts them both in bed together and calls Red Cross to see the falseness of his lady. This time the deception works, probably because the first attempt had sown the seeds of suspicion in the knight's mind. Believing the disguised spirit to be Una, he is with difficulty prevented from drawing his sword upon the two. Restrained from this, he mounts his horse and leaves, taking the dwarf with him. Thus the forces of evil, which Spenser identifies by unmistakable signs as the forces of Rome, have separated the Christian champion from the true faith—or, in terms of national allegory, the English Christian (he is later called St. George) from the Protestant Church of England. This separation is essential to both plot and allegory. Once Red Cross is separated from Una, who was his spiritual inspiration as well as his ladylove, trouble begins for both of them. Lacking true religion, Red Cross is led astray by the temptations of lust and pride; deprived of the protective strength of her knight, Una falls a prey to wicked men.

The events we have just predicted occupy the major part of the book, Cantos 2–8. Although Spenser breaks them up for variety, we will here follow through each career continuously. Of the two, Red Cross's adventures are much more important. For Una it was only necessary that she be kept from rejoining her knight until the proper time. Taking advantage of the old theme of love "on the rebound," Spenser immediately provides Red Cross with an opportunity to become infatuated with the witch Duessa. When operating among her enemies, Duessa takes the name of Fidessa and the form of a rather flashily beautiful damsel. She is thus the exact opposite of Una, for she pretends to be true faith by her name and true beauty by her

appearance, but both are false. This parallel opposition is
a favorite device with Spenser. We have already seen an
example of it in the true and false Florimels of Books III–
V. Following his practice in this book of warning his
readers but not his characters, Spenser immediately introduces the ironic incident of Fradubio. Having acquired
Duessa, as we shall call her, by the overthrow of the Saracen knight Sans Foy, Red Cross is soon engaged in dal-
liance with her and reaches up to pluck some branches
from a tree in order to weave a garland. To his horror the
tree objects in human speech. Fradubio, once a man and
now a tree, tells a pitiful story of how a certain Duessa
had caused him to prefer her to his former lady and how,
when he discovered that she was a loathsome witch in disguise, she transformed both him and his lady into the two
trees under which the knight is sitting. Though somewhat
sobered by this tale, the latter sees no connection with his
own situation and makes no objection to going to the court
of Queen Lucifera with Duessa. This court is held in the
famous House of Pride. In a stately palace of brick and
golden foil, with many fair windows and galleries, obviously modeled on Hampton Court, the great queen holds
audience, surrounded by "a noble crew of Lordes and
Ladies, which with their presence fair the place much
beautifide." The scene that follows is one of the most brilliant in the whole *Faerie Queene* and deserves liberal quo-
tation:

> High above all a cloth of state was spred,
> And a rich throne, as bright as sunny day,
> On which there sate most brave embellished
> With royal robes and gorgeous array,
> A mayden queene, that shone as Titan's ray,
> In glistering gold, and peereless pretious stone:
> Yet her bright blazing beauty did assay

To dim the brightnesse of her glorious throne,
As envying herselfe, that too exceeding shone.

So proud she shined in her princely state,
Looking to heaven; for earth she did disdayne,
And sitting high; for lowly she did hate:
Lo underneath her scornefull feete was layne
A dreadfull dragon with an hideous trayne
And in her hand she held a mirrhour bright,
Wherein her face she often vewed fayne,
And in her self-lov'd semblance tooke delight;
For she was wondrous faire, as any living wight.

And proud Lucifera men did her call,
That made herself a queene, and crownd to be,
Yet rightfull kingdome she had none at all,
Ne heritage of native soveraintie,
But did usurpe with wrong and tyrannie
Upon the scepter which she now did hold:
Ne ruled her realmes with lawes, but pollicie,
And strong advisement of six wisards old,
That with their counsels bad her kingdome did uphold.

By copying his palace from Hampton Court and by referring to Lucifera as a maiden queen Spenser daringly invites comparison with his own sovereign, but by the use
of the dragon (compare the appearance of the lion in a
similar position in the parallel description of Mercilla's
court in Book V, Canto 9) and the statement of usurped
rule he makes it clear that this maiden queen is the antith-
esis of Elizabeth, that she apes with unbecoming haughtiness the magnificence of the true Elizabeth.

Red Cross and Duessa are led in by the usher, Vanitie,
and receive a disdainful greeting from the Queen of Pride.
The courtiers, on the other hand, glad of a chance to show
off before strangers, welcome them most politely:

Her lordes and ladies all this while devise
Themselves to setten forth to straungers' sight:

The Allegorist

Some frounce their curled haire in courtly guise,
Some prancke their ruffes, and others trimly dight
Their gay attire: each others greater pride does spight.

The six counselors mentioned in the description of Lucifera are, of course, the other six of the seven deadly sins,
pride having always ranked as the chief of sins. They are
described in lavish detail. No sooner is the description
finished than Sans Joy, brother of the Sans Foy in whose
company Red Cross had found Duessa, comes into court
and attacks Red Cross even in the royal presence. Repri-
manded by the queen, he demands vengeance for the death
of his brother and throws down his gauntlet. The next day
Red Cross mortally wounds his foe; and, filled with pride
in himself, he falls before Lucifera "on lowly knee to
make her present of his service seene," forgetting in his
worship of her seeming majesty that he had once pledged
allegiance to Gloriana.

While Red Cross is recovering from his wounds, the
dwarf does a little snooping around. He discovers that this
gorgeous palace contains a loathsome dungeon full of
great kings and famous ladies who had mortgaged their
lives to Pride, Wrath, and Envy. The passage is a notable
showpiece, in which Spenser contributes his bit to the long
traditon of *ubi sunt* poetry. Nor is it out of place. The
House of Pride is exactly where we should see that the
path of tyranny leads to an eternal dungeon. The effect of
this upon the knight is to give him his first taste of fear.
This is not an enemy who can be fought by arms; it is
some evil power hanging over the palace he is in. With his
wounds half healed, he gathers up his armor and flies by
night. As soon as Duessa discovers his departure, she sets
out after him, determined that he shall not escape her
clutches. Before long she finds him disarmed, resting be-

side a spring in the shade. Still suspecting nothing of Duessa's true nature, Red Cross begins again to make love to her. He is suddenly interrupted by the appearance of a terrible giant named Orgoglio (Pride), who captures the weakened and unarmed knight without even a fight. At the request of Duessa, Orgoglio spares his life but throws him into a deep dungeon instead. To this ignominious end has come the champion who by his virtue was to have rescued Una's parents from a great dragon. The Christian man, having lost the spiritual guidance of the true faith, has given way to successive temptations of pride and lust. Seduced by the sex appeal of Duessa and by undue confidence in his own powers because of his two victories, he becomes oblivious to moral dangers until it is too late. His flight from the palace was not the result of a true understanding of the danger of pride as the sin which opens the way to all other sins but only of unreasoning fright. The very fact that a formerly brave and hitherto victorious knight falls a prey to sudden terror shows how far his character has been undermined. The same thing is indicated by his unarmed condition at the time of his capture, for Spenser has told us in the letter to Sir Walter Raleigh that his armor is the armor of a Christian man as described by St. Paul. Because of the allurements of pride and lust, he has ceased to practice the Christian virtues and thus is without moral vigor to defend himself.

When Milton, who was a great admirer of Spenser's works, wrote that if virtue were feeble heaven itself would stoop to her, he might have had Red Cross and Una in mind. Although her knight has deserted her, Una never loses faith in him, and it is her persistent loving search which eventually brings about his recovery. Traveling alone after leaving the hermitage of Archimago, she is

captured by Sans Loy, the third of the three Saracen
brothers. His attempt to rape her is prevented by the
tumultuous arrival of a great crowd of fauns and satyrs
brought to the scene by her cries. They drive off the rav-
isher by force of numbers and convey Una to old Sylvanus,
where all the "woodborne people" worship her as a goddess:

> They all as glad as birds of joyous prime
> Thence lead her forth, about her dancing round,
> Shouting and singing all a shepherds' ryme,
> And with greene braunches strowing all the ground,
> Do worship her as queene with olive girlond crownd.
>
> And all the way their merry pipes they sound,
> That all the woods with doubled eccho ring,
> And with their horned feet do weare the ground,
> Leaping like wanton kids in pleasant spring.
> So towards old Sylvanus they her bring;
> Who with the noise awaked, cometh out,
> To weet the cause, his weak steps governing
> And aged limbs on cypresse stadle stout,
> And with an ivy twyne his wast is girt about.
>
> Far off he wonders what them makes so glad
> Or Bacchus merry fruit they did invent.
> Or Cybele's franticke rites have made them mad;
> They drawing nigh, unto their god present
> That flowre of faith and beautie excellent.
> The god himselfe, vewing that mirrhour rare,
> Stood long amazd, and burnt in his intent;
> His owne faire Dryope now he thinks not faire,
> And Pholoe fowle, when her to this he doth compare.
>
> The woodborne people fall before her flat,
> And worship her as goddesse of the wood;
> And old Sylvanus selfe bethinkes not what
> To thinke of wight so faire, but gazing stood,
> In doubt to deeme her borne of earthly brood;
> Sometimes Dame Venus selfe he seemes to see,

[113]

> But Venus never had so sober mood;
> Sometimes Diana he her takes to bee,
> But misseth bow and shaftes and buskins to her knee.

> The woody nymphes, faire hamadryades,
> Her to behold do thither runne apace,
> And all the troupe of light-foot naiades
> Flocke all about to see her lovely face;
> But when they vewed have her heavenly grace,
> They envie her in their malitious mind,
> And fly away for feare of fowle disgrace:
> But all the satyres scorne their woody kind,
> And henceforth nothing faire but her on earth they find.

Here is the parallel to the House of Pride, set in the beauty and simplicity of nature instead of in the gilded trappings of Lucifera's court. Instead of the self-centered courtiers, intent on showing off their own elegance, we have the untutored amazement of the "woody kind" of ancient mythology. Red Cross, even though welcomed haughtily by Lucifera, fell more and more into the sin of pride; Una, though worshiped as a goddess, tries throughout her stay with these simple creatures to put aside their idolatry and teach them true religion.

Una's release from the satyrs is brought about by one of the most interesting knights in the *Faerie Queene*, Sir Satyrane. Son of a human mother and a satyr father, by whom he is brought up to force wild animals to do his will, Satyrane is a sort of Elizabethan Mowgli. Taking away a lioness's cubs and riding upon the backs of wild bulls are among his common amusements. Later, being desirous of fame, he undertook knight-errantry.—

> And far abroad for strange adventures sought,
> In which his might was never overthrowne,
> But through all Faery lond his famous worth was blown.

The Allegorist

Coming back to the woods to revisit his satyr relatives, he finds Una teaching true religion to them as they sit around her. Attracted to both her person and her doctrine, he offers her his aid. They escape from the satyrs, only to be attacked again by Sans Loy. While Satyrane is exchanging blows with him, Una continues her flight alone.

At this point the separated plot of Book I reunites, for the next person met by Una is her dwarf, who had escaped when the Red Cross Knight was captured by Orgoglio. He tells her the story of all that has gone on since the separation, and it is in the very midst of her despair and grief that the heaven-sent figure of Prince Arthur arrives in all his splendor. His glittering armor, studded with jewels, shines from afar. His shield is a single mass of diamond, endowed with magic properties, which can turn men to stone and therefore is ordinarily covered. With him is his beloved squire, carrying his lance. Since Arthur represents a mission of divine love carrying grace to mankind—we should remember that in the following scene he takes the part assigned to the Savior in the Revelation of St. John—it is worth noticing that the idea of love for an erring mortal has been stressed just before his arrival in the stanza describing Una's grief:

> And love fresh coles unto her fire did lay,
> For greater love, the greater is the losse.
> Was never Ladie loved dearer day,
> Then she did love the knight of the Redcrosse,
> For whose dear sake so many troubles her did tosse.

Since Una stands not only for true faith in the abstract but also for the visible church on earth, we have here the allegory of the church yearning for the fallen sinner at the very moment when the grace of God is about to rescue him.

Una now relates to Arthur not only her present need but also the history of her parents, who have sent her out to obtain aid for them. They are the king and queen of the Garden of Eden (obviously Adam and Eve as representative of the human race) and are besieged by a great dragon who has already destroyed many knights who have attempted the rescue. At length she came to Gloriana's court, where the Red Cross Knight was assigned to her.

Led by the dwarf, Una and her new protector come to the castle of Orgoglio, who issues forth to battle accompanied by Duessa riding on a seven-headed beast. Arthur and his squire are nearly defeated by this terrible combination of enemies. The giant's last and most crushing blow knocks Arthur flat on the ground, but in doing so it tears the cover from his shield, whose magic power puts an end to the conflict. Thus are we reminded that God uses human agents, but the victory is his alone. Orgoglio is killed and Duessa given in charge to the squire. When Red Cross has been pulled out of his filthy dungeon by Arthur's own efforts ("Entire affection hateth nicer hands," Spenser says), he is welcomed with joyful tears by Una. The whole party returns to the courtyard, where she insists that Duessa be stripped so that her real ugliness may be brought home to all concerned. The evil work of deception must be thoroughly undone. The passage which follows shows that Spenser could describe foulness with quite as much gusto as beauty when occasion required.

A lesser genius than Spenser's would have sent Red Cross on to slay the great dragon as soon as his strength was recovered. It is exactly at this point that Spenser's psychological insight is most acute. He realized that during the knight's long imprisonment his spiritual strength must have waned along with his physical strength. Mor-

bidly aware of his sins against both God and his lady, he is
in no danger of falling a prey to Duessa's charms again,
but temptations of another sort he is ill equipped to resist.
After leaving Arthur at the beginning of Canto 9 with an
exchange of symbolic gifts, Una and Red Cross see approaching them an unarmed knight, with a rope around
his neck, trembling with fear. He tells them that he has
just escaped in the nick of time from "a man of hell, that
calls himselfe Despaire," who was persuading him to kill
himself. Red Cross, not yet free from pride of intellect,
scoffs at him and says that he will not rest until he has
heard and tried that traitor's art. Despair's dwelling is not
hard to find. Dark and doleful as a greedy grave, it lies
under a craggy cliff surrounded by ragged stubs of dead
trees. Outside the cave is the bleeding corpse of his last
suicide victim. When Red Cross accuses him of the crime,
he expresses surprise. He maintains that he has done the
man a favor by helping him to find eternal rest and happy
ease in the next world. Red Cross fails to note the fallacy
in this argument (naturally one guilty of the sin of suicide
would find no such thing in the next world) and tries to
enter into debate with Despair. The latter rapidly over-
whelms him with specious false statements, ending with a
powerful appeal to the knight's sense of his own recent
sins:

> Thou, wretched man, of death hast greatest need,
> If in true balance thou wilt weigh thy state
> For never knight that dared warlike deede
> More lucklesse disavantures did amate:
> Witnesse the dongeon deepe, wherein of late
> Thy life shut up for death so oft did call;
> And through good lucke prolonged hath thy date,
> Yet death then would the like mishaps forestall,
> Into the which hereafter thou mayest happen fall.

Why then doest thou, O man of sin, desire
To draw thy dayes forth to their last degree?
Is not the measure of thy sinful hire
High heaped up with huge iniquitie,
Against the day of wrath to burden thee?
Is not enough, that to this ladie milde
Thou falsed hast thy faith with perjury,
And sold thyself to serve Duessa vilde,
With whom in all abuse thou hast thyself defilde?

Is not he just that all this doth behold
From highest heaven, and bears an equall eye?
Shall he thy sins up in his knowledge fold,
And guiltie be of thine impietie?
Is not his law, Let every sinner die:
Die shall all flesh? what then must needs be donne,
Is it not better to doe willinglie,
Then linger till the glasse be all out ronne?
Death is the end of woes: die soone, O fairies sonne.

Carried away by the emotional force of this appeal, Red
Cross fails to note its denial of the New Testament. His
conscience makes him guilty of everything Despair said;
and when the latter presses a sharp dagger into his hand,
he lifts it up to strike into his own breast. In the fight with
Error it had been enough for Una to cry out to her knight,
"Add faith unto thy force." This time she knows he is in
such desperate need that words will not suffice. Also for
once she is really angry:

Out of his hand she snatcht the cursed knife,
And threw it to the ground, enraged rife,
And to him said, Fie, Fie, faint-harted knight,
What meanest thou by this reprochful strife?
Is this the battell which thou vauntst to fight
With that fire-mouthed dragon, horrible and bright?

Come, come away, fraile, feeble, fleshly wight,
Ne let vaine words bewitch thy manly heart,
Ne divelish thoughts dismay thy constant spright.

The Allegorist

In heavenly mercies hast thou not a part?
Why shouldst thou then despair, that chosen art?
Where justice grows, there grows eke greater grace,
The which doth quench the brond of hellish smart,
And that accurst hand-writing doth deface.
Arise, sir knight, arise, and leave this cursed place.

This well-deserved rebuke is one of Spenser's most vigorous speeches. It is so just in its condemnation, so power-
fully expressed, and withal so very human in its temporary
anger at a loved one that all readers who have been afraid
that Una was too good and gentle to be true feel like
bursting into applause. It is this scene with Despair, not
the battle with Orgoglio, which forms the climax of the
plot. It reminds us of the Radegund incident in Book V,
where again an overconfident knight undertakes to show
an unfortunate fellow-man how to deal with a perilous
situation and then has to be rescued himself by a woman.
Spenser, unlike Milton, had no illusions about the superiority of the male sex.

The Red Cross Knight is now fully aware that he needs
both bodily and spiritual recuperation. He is taken by Una
to the House of Holiness, where the bad effects of the
House of Pride may be corrected. Here he receives instruction in Christian belief from Fidelia and Speranza
(Faith and Hope), in the practice of a Christian life from
Charissa (Love), and in the nature and use of Christian inspiration from the holy hermit Contemplation. This threefold division corresponds to the activities of the three persons of the Trinity. Such a summary may make the House
of Holiness sound too much like a lecture on theology; actually it is not. The spirit of the place is neither abstract
nor dull. Coelia, the mother, is as full of graceful bearing
and courtesy as she is of good works. Two of the daugh-

[119]

ters, betrothed but not yet married, are inseparable companions, "ylinked arme in arme in lovely wise." These are, of course, Faith and Hope. Charissa, the third sister, is married and has many children. As fast as Fidelia makes the knight see his sins in the true light of the Word of God, Speranza prevents him from falling into despair again by giving him the sweet comfort of hope in the mercy and grace extended to man. When his repentance and penance are completed, Una takes him to Charissa. Under her he is taught to perform the seven acts of mercy toward his fellow-men. The whole establishment breathes an air of peace and hope like that of Dante's Purgatory where the souls are filled with joy at the prospect of their approaching fitness for heaven. Red Cross, too, is now in a state of grace and is permitted a vision of the Heavenly City from the mountain lookout of the hermit Contemplation:

> As he thereon stood gazing, he might see
> The blessed angels to and fro descend
> From highest heaven, in gladsome companee,
> And with great joy into that city wend,
> As commonly as friend does with his friend.
> Whereat he wondred much and gan enquere,
> What stately building durst so high extend
> Her lofty towers unto the starry sphere,
> And what unknowen nation there empeopled were.

Informed that it is the New Jerusalem, he conceives such great joy in it that he wishes never to return to earthly life again. The hermit tells him that God must be served on earth as well as in heaven, that he has an unfulfilled quest to perform for Una. He also informs Red Cross that the Faerie Queene, Gloriana, is heavenly born and that men properly serve her on earth for earthly glory until

The Allegorist

such time as they may earn entrance into the higher service of heaven.

We now come to the last two cantos, in which the conquest of the great dragon and the marriage of the hero and heroine are related. Fights, as we have already remarked, are not Spenser's strong point, and this one is no exception. After convincing us through hair-raising description that nothing on earth could stand up against this particular winged dreadnought, Spenser makes the Red Cross Knight do it for three days. The fact that each night he is saved by a miracle does not help the narrative any. For once in this book the allegory gets in the way of a convincing story. The three days were supposed to symbolize the three days of Christ's crucifixion, harrowing of hell, and resurrection, while the two miraculous cures of the half-dead knight represent the efficacy of baptism and the Lord's Supper. Once these supernatural events are out of the way, the narrative regains all its old power. In fact, there is no place in Book I, I think, where it is better:

> Then gan triumphant trompets sound on hie,
> That sent to heaven the echoed report
> Of their new joy and happie victory
> Gainst him that had them long opprest with tort,
> And fast imprisoned in sieged fort.
> Then all the people, as in solemne feast,
> To him assembled with one full consort,
> Rejoycing at the fall of that great beast,
> From whose eternall bondage now they were releast.

Out come the king and queen with their nobles and councilors, out come the young men and maidens with music and dance, and out comes too the "rude rabblement" to gaze upon the dead monster in fearful curiosity. The various comments of the crowd are given with almost Chaucerian gusto. In the meantime the Red Cross Knight is conducted to the palace, where he is thanked by the king and queen. The king brings out Una, who has changed her traveling clothes for fresh white garments which make her beauty shine forth with transcendent brightness. She now symbolizes the church triumphant in heaven, the bride of Christ. The king is about to unite the happy pair when Spenser introduces a most surprising and effective complication of the plot. There is an attempt to forbid the marriage! A breathless messenger rushes into the hall and presents a letter to the king from Duessa claiming that Red Cross was previously betrothed to her. This claim is calculated to do great damage to Red Cross; for, although it is not strictly true, there is enough truth in it to cause him untold embarrassment. Not only may the king refuse his daughter because of the scandal, but Una herself may believe the charge and reject her successful suitor even at the altar in a revulsion of feeling. Nothing, however, can shake her faith and trust in her chosen knight. Interrupting his attempts to explain the situation, she informs her father of the wicked wiles of Duessa and suggests that the messenger is Archimago in disguise, a guess which turns out to be correct. The wedding ceremonies are resumed, and Red Cross and Una are married to the strains of mysterious music,

> Like as it had bene many an angels voice
> Singing before th'eternall majesty,
> In their trinal triplicities on high.

When we look back upon Book I as a whole, it is clear that plot rather than character has been the main concern of the poet; and it is the whole plot, rather than the separate incidents, which is important. The method is the opposite of that of Book III, where the significance lies in a series of different relationships. Therefore we find that the characters are not highly individualized, as in Chaucer or a modern novel, but represent types of humanity. They are well enough portrayed to carry out their parts in the action, but there is no attempt to make them memorable as personalities. To do so would have interfered with the poet's purpose. Everyman must not become too much one particular man; True Faith should not remind you of the girl you used to go around with at college. The plot, on the other hand, has been very carefully worked out to present a clear-cut dramatic story with emotional climaxes and unexpected surprises. The falling of the Red Cross Knight into even more terrible danger immediately after his rescue by Arthur and the last-minute attempt of Duessa to interrupt her rival's marriage are highly ingenious and satisfying. There is a constant but unobtrusive use of parallelism. Una is opposed to Duessa; the false holiness of the hermit Archimago is balanced by the true holiness of the hermit Contemplation; the work of the House of Pride is undone by that of the House of Holiness; and, finally, Lucifera is the opposite of Gloriana. There is much of this subtle balancing of forces which reveals itself only upon repeated readings of the story.

What is true of the narrative structure is equally true of the allegorical structure, which is the most elaborate and most satisfactory of the whole six books. It is the most satisfactory because, if properly interpreted, it is the clearest. To understand the meaning, it is necessary to remember what we learned about Spenser's methods in chapter iii. He is more concerned to make his moral attitude clear than he is to identify particular persons or events of the real world with persons and events in the story. Furthermore, a character in the story may not always bear the same interpretation in different scenes, but the scene itself almost always makes the proper interpretation clear.

Fundamental to the allegory of the whole *Faerie Queene* is the conception of the three different levels of meaning. First, there is the moral or religious meaning, which is always the most important to the general structure. Second, there is the national allegory. This involves such identifications as Red Cross standing for England or the English people and his opponents standing for various enemies of England. Third, there is personal allegory. This is often purely episodic, and much confusion can be caused by trying to make it systematic throughout a whole book or the whole poem. For instance, when Duessa is tried and executed for treason against Mercilla in Book V, it is obvious that she is Mary of Scotland—so obvious that her son James entered a diplomatic protest—but it is quite unnecessary to seek for parallels to Mary's life in all of Duessa's actions. Arthur's squire has not even a name in Books I and II; in Books III and IV he is called Timias and is quite obviously Sir Walter Raleigh. Finally, we must beware of thinking that Spenser is always operating simultaneously on all these three levels. Outside of Book I this hardly ever happens, and even in Book I it by no means happens all the time.

To make these principles clearer, let us take the three main characters (Red Cross, Una, and Duessa) and see how the allegory works out. Red Cross is, first of all, the Christian man seeking holiness; second, as St. George, he is England. Una is the one true faith, which on the second level is the Church of England. Since Elizabeth was by law the head of the church, Una also at times stands for Elizabeth. Duessa is "doubleness" or deception; her outstand-

ing quality is the falseness of everything she seems or pro-
fesses. On the national level she figures, as the daughter
of the great emperor on the Tiber (the pope), along with
Archimago, as a representative of the Roman church and
its chief national ally, Spain. Last, as we have said, she is
at certain points Mary of Scotland. In Book I this occurs
when she makes her claim on England in the person of the
Red Cross Knight in the twelfth canto. In this scene, Una
of course, is Elizabeth. Many scholars formerly thought
that Book I was a detailed allegory of the history of the
English reformation in which each character could be identified with some sixteenth-century figure. Such an interpretation is too literalistic and is full of dangers. Carried
out logically, it would involve such absurdities as maintaining that Una's parents stand for Henry VIII and Anne
Boleyn. The religious allegory of Book I is remarkably
full and logical; the national and personal allegories are incidental. Take, for instance, the conclusion of the poem.
The killing of the dragon is the conquest of Satan, or sin,
by the Christian man with the assistance of the two divine
sacraments recognized by the Church of England. Still in
the religious sphere, it may be interpreted as the victory of
Christ over death and hell. There is no national or personal
significance here. The union of Red Cross and Una means
the attainment of holiness by a Christian or, on the other
hand, the marriage of Christ and the church. On the national level it signifies the acceptance of the Protestant
faith by the English people under Elizabeth. And on the
personal level there is the claim of Mary Stuart to Elizabeth's throne. This last is an excellent plot device but has
no connection with the moral allegory, unless to show that
old sins can always crop up to hurt us.

From these main points it is easy enough to follow the

allegorical meaning of the action in Book I. Its theme is the Christian life, with its struggle against sin, and as such it is intended for Christian readers. The more such readers are aware of the traditional beliefs and symbolism of their religion the more they will recognize and appreciate the extraordinary richness and detail of Spenser's allegorical structure. The main points of it are so soundly based on human psychology that it can be construed by anyone as a treatment of man's moral life in this world, whatever his views may be about God and the next world.

Although Book II has had its admirers, most readers find it disappointing when contrasted either with the unified plot allegory of Book I or with the diversified and interwoven situations of Book III. It contains irrelevant matter involving characters who are to appear later in the poem but who seem to have no connection with the action of this book. Its two most striking allegorical structures, the House of Medina and the House of Temperance, are not only relatively uninteresting but are unnecessary to the moral training of the hero. The House of Temperance might have been given a significant place in the story of Guyon were it not that Arthur is allowed to usurp the principal interest just at this point. On the other hand, Book II is not without compensating virtues. It contains some of the best fights in the *Faerie Queene*, some excellent incidental lyrics, and a most engaging minor character named Phaedria. It also contains the most famous of all Spenser's showpieces, the Bower of Bliss. No one could wish a piece of work with so many excellences unwritten; but it is permitted to wish that it could have received the thoughtful attention from its author which produced such a masterpiece of logical structure in Book I.

The Allegorist

Because of its lack of coherence, the plot of Book II does not merit the detailed analysis given to that of Book I. It seems desirable, however, to assist the reader by a summary of the action. The beginning of Guyon's quest is related in Canto 1 when he comes across some tragic victims of the malice of the enchantress Acrasia. The alternative explanation in Canto 2 that the palmer came to Gloriana's court asking for a knight may be dismissed as an incomplete attempt to revise the book in accord with a plan centered in Gloriana's annual feast. The account of Medina and her two sisters, illustrative of the golden mean and the Aristotelian conception of virtue, does not advance the plot at all. Canto 3 is devoted to an entirely irrelevant account of a meeting between Belphoebe and Braggadochio. This introduction of characters belonging to Books III–V, justified only by the fact that Braggadochio has stolen Guyon's horse, is a rather inexpert attempt to link together the books of the *Faerie Queene*. Cantos 4–8 form the center of the action. Furor and Occasion are defeated and bound by Guyon. Soon after, he meets and overcomes the fiery tempered Pyrocles, whose attendant is Atin, the spirit of strife. Pyrocles, on being granted his life, begs Guyon to release Furor and Occasion. When the latter rather foolishly does this, they both seize upon Pyrocles and give him a beating. Atin hastens to the Bower of Bliss to get Cymocles, Pyrocles' brother, to recsue him. Canto 6 contains an interesting crisscross action in which Guyon, in search of the Bower of Bliss, and Cymocles, hastening away from it, meet each other on an island belonging to one of Acrasia's adherents, a girl named Phaedria. She is called by Spenser the spirit of immodest mirth. She laughs, talks, and giggles all the time. Life never bores her; she never tires of the sound of her own voice. We have all met

[127]

her at parties and on the beach. She welcomes Cymocles as a fellow-servant of Acrasia but refuses to take Atin into her little boat. Similarly, she is glad to receive a handsome knight like Guyon but excludes the sober aged palmer. When the two men meet on Phaedria's island, Cymocles immediately flares up and accuses Guyon of being responsible for his brother's plight. The angry fight which ensues is broken up by Phaedria. Excessive mirth may be a fault, but it will not tolerate anger because that spoils the enjoyment of life. Spenser even stops to praise this garrulous little enemy of temperance because she shows the power "of courteous clemencie in gentle heart." Seeing that Guyon is a foe to folly, Phaedria gladly ferries him to the other side of the lake, where he continues his quest.

The temptations of Mammon, elaborately described in a long trip through the underworld, form the next adventure. Though an excellent piece of narrative, it suffers from two defects: there are too many scenes in it, and it is too obvious that Guyon feels no desire for riches or ambition. In fact, he says as much at the beginning of the canto but nevertheless accompanies Mammon upon the flimsy excuse that he wants to see where Mammon's gold comes from. Not only is Guyon not the kind of person to be attracted by material wealth, but in addition to this, Spenser makes it impossible for him to show any leanings in that direction. The moment he enters the gate of Mammon's underworld kingdom a grisly fiend steps in behind him,

> The which with monstrous stalke behind him stept
> And ever as he went, due watch upon him kept.
>
> Well hoped he, ere long that hardy guest,
> If ever covetous hand or lustfull eye,
> Or lips he layd on thing that likt him best,
> Or ever sleepe his eye-strings did untye,

Should be his prey. And therefore still on hye
He over him did hold his cruell clawes,
Threatening with greedy gripe to do him dye
And rend in peeces with his ravenous pawes,
If ever he transgrest the fatall Stygian lawes.

Since the slightest mental slip means death, it is impossible
for Spenser to show any moral struggle going on within
the hero's mind. Yet without moral struggle the whole episode lacks significance. In the Bower of Bliss, Spenser does
not make this mistake.

In Canto 8 Spenser's plan called for the usual rescue by
Arthur. Now it is evident that Guyon, far from needing
rescue, has vanquished all his foes and resisted the temptations of Mammon. The palmer, we must remember, has
been separated from him by Phaedria. This lack of support from his moral guide and the fact that the three-day
tour of the lower world was performed by him without
food or sleep was sufficient excuse for him to fall into a
dead faint on his return to the upper air. The palmer turns
up again but is powerless to prevent Pyrocles and Cymocles from robbing what they suppose to be a corpse. At
this moment Arthur arrives and undertakes to recover the
armor. This leads to one of Spenser's best combats, in
which Arthur breaks his own weapons and is able to win
only when the palmer runs to him with Guyon's sword.
The sword of Temperance himself was necessary to subdue these types of violent intemperance. After this, according to the usual plan, Arthur should have gone his own
way as soon as the proper thanks and chivalric amenities
had been attended to. In Book II, however, he does not do
this but remains to dominate the next three cantos, interrupting the main plot and interfering with the allegory.
The only reasonable explanation of this change is that

Spenser, at the time he finally put the material of Book II together, decided that Arthur, as the announced hero of the *Faerie Queene* as a whole, ought to play a larger part. If this explanation is true, we can see that he was not pleased with the result, for he never again allowed Arthur such a prominent place.

Arthur and Guyon go to the House of Temperance. This rather naïvely allegorical structure has apartments representing the various parts of the human body and its mental faculties. It is presided over by Alma, the soul. Unlike the House of Holiness, the House of Temperance is not necessary to Guyon's future success. On the other hand, standing for the human body, it needs a protector against the dangerous temptations of the five senses. Guyon, who stands for Temperance, should obviously have been this protector, if the allegory is to be in harmony with the plot. Instead Spenser sends him off in a hurry to the Bower of Bliss, accompanied by his palmer, leaving Arthur to fight with Maleger and his horde of savages. This is an even more arduous battle than the previous one with Pyrocles and Cymocles, but with the timely aid of his squire he finally kills Maleger and returns in triumph to Alma.

Guyon and the palmer in the meantime have continued their pursuit of Acrasia. After an arduous marine voyage, in which they avoid or overcome many allegorical dangers, they are put ashore at the Bower of Bliss. The incidents which follow, in the last half of Canto 12, are among the most famous in the *Faerie Queene* and form a passage of magnificent poetry. They have also been used to support attacks on Spenser's integrity as a thinker and a moralist. Here is the evidence, critics of this school say, that Spenser's praise of temperance and chastity is insincere, that he really enjoyed sensual description and luscious immoral incidents and only put in the morality as a sop to convention. The complete answer to such an interpretation, which seems to me to be based on a strange misconception of the whole meaning of the *Faerie Queene*, has been given by C. S. Lewis in his book, *The Allegory of Love*. What I shall say here owes much to him. First of all, let us remember what we have been told in the poem about the Bower of Bliss before arriving at it. At the very beginning of Book II we were presented with the tragic fate of a man who had fallen prey to the pleasures offered by Acrasia. He had discovered that her love could quickly turn to deadly hate and to murder. Again, in Canto 5, we discover that Cymocles, one of the chief villains of the story, lives in the Bower of Bliss. By these clearly unmistakable signs Spenser has warned us that the seeming beauty of the Bower, as of its mistress, is only an artful disguise. The pleasure to be found there will not be recreative pleasure, good for the health of body and mind, but will be quite the opposite. Its pleasure will make soft weaklings out of strong men and will corrupt the mind and understanding so that the truth can no longer be discerned. This meaning indeed is so obvious that it is hard to see how any reader could fail to understand it. The difficulty seems to be that Spenser makes the temptations of the Bower real temptations. He makes it clear that these snares of the flesh are attractions to shake the stability of men previously quite confident of their virtue.

The strength of these temptations has long been attested by the titillations of delight which all readers experience as they accompany Guyon and the palmer in the dangerous exploit of capturing the enchantress in the midst of her own bower (one is tempted to say "boudoir"). At the gate Genius—Spenser explains that he is our evil genius, that is, the tempter within us—offers wine, an offer repeated shortly after by Excess, a beautiful woman in loose, disarranged garments. Guyon is not much tempted by intoxication of this kind, but when he comes to a pool where two naked girls are wantonly disporting themselves to attract his attention, the palmer "much rebukt those wandring eyes of his" and dragged him along. This, I think, is the one place where the reader has a legitimate complaint. Thinking of poor Red Cross's helplessness when exposed to the charms of Duessa, he wants to know what Guyon would have done if the palmer had not been there. However, the palmer, whom we must never forget to be the personification of reason, *is* there, and the two proceed to the place where Acrasia, in as near as possible to a naked state, is fondling the head of a young recreant knight (delightfully named Verdant!) in her lap while an attendant hidden in the background sings a beautiful song about the rose. His warlike arms hang idle on a tree near by. Undoubtedly this young knight, with his idle arms, reminded Guyon of the knight destroyed by Acrasia in Canto 1 and renewed his desire to avenge that unfortunate one. Also Acrasia, unlike the damsels in the pool, is occupied and consequently does not offer a personal temptation. He and the palmer rush in, capture Acrasia, and send Verdant home with some good advice. The Bower of Bliss, with all its charming appurtenances, is destroyed. Guyon, more than any other knight except Britomart, has entirely accomplished his quest.

In considering the meaning of all this, we are in a better position than most readers because of our unorthodox beginning of the *Faerie Queene* with Book III. Book III is a symphony in praise of true, honorable love. According to

Spenser such love is to be sought, and when found it is healthy for mind and body. It desires to be fruitful. Therefore in the physical realm it seeks marriage and children, and in the spiritual realm it seeks friendship and acts of generosity, mercy, and justice. It is a thing in which the whole nature of man has part: body, mind, and soul. Such love is a constructive force.

Now Acrasia, with her whole Bower of Bliss, is a destructive force. She does not fulfil men's lives; she wrecks them. Like Circe, she turns her lovers into beasts; if they escape her, she plots to kill them. The confusion of criticism has arisen from a consideration of her enticements without any consideration of what they lead to. There is no difference in *physical* attraction between the bodily beauty of a good woman and a bad woman. Nature has arranged things so that either one will arouse a physical desire for sexual intercourse. It is what such intercourse leads to that the allegory of the Bower of Bliss is concerned with. Although I believe that Spenser probably disapproved of all extra-marital intercourse, that is not what he is talking about here. Acrasia does not stand for mere youthful incontinence nor does she stand for mere occasional infidelity to the marriage vow. She is that kind of sexual passion which seizes upon a man's whole life and destroys it. She represents the temptation to allow bodily pleasure to become an end in itself, to become in fact the chief end of life. More important still, Mr. Lewis has pointed out that the keynote of the Bower is artificiality. Cunning craftsmen, not nature, have produced its decorative effects. There is no fruition there. Cymocles is represented as a Peeping Tom, not as a lover. Acrasia and her bathing girls are not there in order to fall in love with anyone but simply as procurement agents for the increase of her Circean menagerie. This drugging of the mind by giving one's self up to bodily pleasure is partly akin to that desire to throw off responsibility for the problems of life in order to recover a sort of state of primal innocence which is part of primitivism. If we are animals, this temptation says to us, why not act just as our bodies prompt us to? Nature never intended us to surround ourselves with all these restraints and moral laws. In carrying out freely the dictates of our animal nature we shall achieve happiness and rest. Dorothy Sayers has illustrated this temptation and its results in the Helen of Troy motif in her modern Faust play, *The Devil To Pay*. It is interesting that she comes to the same conclusion that Spenser did. Such an irresponsible surrender to sensuality leads only to cruelty and self-destruction. In becoming human instead of animal, man has lost the guidance of natural instinct, which keeps the animals true to their nature and purpose, and must discipline himself in order to achieve any permanently desirable ends.

This temptation to evade the responsibilities of life was not unknown to Spenser. He described it twice in Book I in the spiritual sphere. Red Cross first almost commits suicide in order to escape the struggle with sin. Then, when he is given a vision of the New Jerusalem after the cleansing of his soul in the House of Holiness, he again desires to cease the struggle of life and to enter immediately into the bliss of heaven. In both cases he is informed that he has duties to perform on earth. In the Bower of Bliss, and to a minor degree in the island of Phaedria, this temptation is transferred from the spiritual to the sensual sphere. Those who enjoy the bodily delights of Acrasia really do become animals; but instead of being happy, contented animals they are an ugly, snarling, vicious pack of

[134]

wild beasts. When the palmer restores them to human form, only the hog wishes to remain an animal.

It is curious that we have not recognized Acrasia before. She is the Dark Lady of the sonnets, who came so close to wrecking Shakespeare's life; she is Balzac's Valérie Marneff; she is the kind of love described by Bacon in his essay on that subject. But she is not Chaucer's Cressida, nor is she any manifestation of mankind's desire for union with a loved one, whether or not legalized by marriage. In terms of Spenser's imaginary world she is the absolute opposite of Britomart and Amoret. It is at this point that we realize that the lack of a heroine is a defect in Book II. In making this contrast between constructive and destructive use of sex, between fruitful and unfruitful love, Spenser has deprived himself of a symbol of true fruition. The story of the Red Cross Knight's struggle with pride and error would have lost much of its appeal as well as much of its meaning had there been no personification of truth in it. Britomart's yearning for her lover might have seemed merely schoolgirl sentimentality if she had never found him in Arthegal. We need an Amoret here to show the healthiness of true love and to keep poor Guyon from appearing too much of a negative moralist. If we knew that he had a strong desire for someone who was waiting to be united with him at the end of his quest, we would feel better about his unwilling departure from those girls romping in the pool, even though we may agree with Mr. Lewis that their names were probably Cissie and Flossie. It is true that Guyon told Mammon that he could not accept the latter's offer of his daughter because he was already engaged, but this sounds a good deal like a made-up excuse. We hear nothing else of this supposed betrothal.

The lack of a heroine is only one example of the major

defect of Book II, its failure to unite convincingly plot, character, and allegory. The unfortunate effect of this upon the story has already been shown. We may conclude by observing its effect upon the character of Guyon. We noticed in Book V that Arthegal as a personality suffered from the separation of part of the quality of justice into the figure of Talus. Guyon is the victim of an even more disastrous divorce. In the scheme of Book II Spenser wished to point out that temperance must be accompanied and directed by reason. As long as this idea remains abstract, all is well; but when the abstract ideas are translated into characters in the story, trouble arises. We all agree that in our own lives temperance will be best achieved by using reason to keep our appetites where they belong, but we think of these qualities as parts of a single personality. When, however, Reason becomes a palmer, quite a separate person from Sir Guyon as Temperance, we feel an impairment of Guyon's character. He seems to need good advice too often, and yet he is made out to be a man with practically no wrong desires. If he were really in danger of being carried away by anger, gluttony, avarice, or worldly ambition, we would appreciate the presence of the guiding hand. An incident like Una's rescue of Red Cross from Despair would make the palmer seem more useful. The mechanical unreality of this separation is most annoying in the Bower of Bliss. If Guyon is the great example of a temperate man, we say to ourselves, for heaven's sake let him meet these bathing beauties on his own with no frigid old man around to shake a menacing finger at him. Now, of course, Spenser means all the time that this quality of reason is in Guyon's mind, and for some kinds of allegory this personification might turn out well enough. It does not turn out well in the *Faerie Queene* pre-

cisely because the *Faerie Queene*, in spite of its chivalric
setting, is too real. Red Cross, Satyrane, Britomart, Amoret, Florimel, Hellenore, Paridell, Arthegal, and their friends
are real people to us in spite of their strange clothes, and
we expect them to act like real people with undivided
selves instead of needing a telephone call from some part
of themselves which is masquerading as another person.
Nine times out of ten they do act like real people. This is
because Spenser usually spent a good deal of care in ad-
justing the conflicting claims of plot and allegory in handling his characters. Almost always his care was rewarded
by a reasonable degree of success, as we can easily con-
vince ourselves if we will compare the *Faerie Queene* with
any other large allegorical narrative, but there were times
when his busy life as a public official simply did not allow
for thorough reconsideration of an artistic problem. The
character of Guyon was the greatest loser from this lack
of leisure.

CHAPTER VI

PASTORALISM GLORIFIED
(*Faerie Queene*, VI)

IT IS a pity that so few readers ever reach the last book of the *Faerie Queene*, for in many respects it is the best. Although it has not the superb plot construction of Book I, its sheer narrative power is unsurpassed. It is full of striking contrasts, of subtly blended lights and shades, and of romantic coloring. Pirates, cannibals, hermits, noble savages, and wild bears with babies in their mouths jostle each other in kaleidoscopic procession along with the usual knights-errant and ladies in distress. More than this, it is closer than any of the other books to the great world of outdoor nature. It breathes of the woods and the fields, and it gives a picture of idealized pastoral life so charming that its hero is seduced away from the duty of his quest for a long delightful truancy. It is here that the early, sometimes crude, pastoralism of the *Shepherds' Calendar* reasserts itself in great poetry.

The freshness and enthusiasm of the narrative owes a great deal to the position of Book VI in the poem. It is a new lease on life for the poet's imagination. He has finished at last with the extended plots of the previous group of books and is now free to take any way he pleases through "this delightful land of faery." The opening stanza of the prologue is full of joy in the sweet variety which lies before him. The characters, with the exception of Arthur and Timias, are all new, and a very attractive lot they are. Although there are no major creations like

[138]

Britomart among them, they have an air of freshness and spontaneity about them quite unlike the woodenness of many of the figures in Books II and V. It is also greatly to their credit that they do not merely repeat the types of earlier successful characters. Tristram may be technically a variant of Satyrane, but he does not remind us of the latter's personality; and the same may be said of Calepine's relation to Scudamour. Crudor and Turpine are better than the previous stock villains, and Turpine's wife, Blandina, has the makings of a very suave and skilful villainess who could have been developed in later books if the author had lived. The pirate chief and the cannibal priest are new types.

The hero's quest, the pursuit of the Blatant Beast, is given greater prominence than usual, but more as narrative than as allegory. Its moral significance is not so full and central as that of Britomart's quest or Guyon's or the Red Cross Knight's. The reason for this is not far to seek. Courtesy is a different kind of virtue from holiness, temperance, or chastity. It is vaguer and more diffuse in its manifestations, harder to isolate and clarify in terms of doctrine. The Beast represents malice and slander, the breaking of the Ninth Commandment, obviously an important enemy of the courteous man but by no means the only enemy, as the other incidents show. Spenser is therefore obliged by the very nature of his moral theme to branch out into that variety of narrative upon which we have been commenting. Plot and allegory are in accord here just as they are in Books I and III.

The structure of Book VI breaks very neatly into three parts. The first two cantos contain isolated incidents illustrating Calidore's courtesy. Cantos 3–8 contain the story of Calepine and Serena, intermingled first with Calidore

and later with Arthur. Cantos 9–12 deal with Calidore's
love for Pastorella, his rescue of her, and his conquest of
the Blatant Beast. The first two cantos deal with incidents
involving cruelty and inhumanity. Briana's evil custom of
demanding the hair of ladies and the beards of knights who
pass her castle is shown to have originated in a demand
made upon her by a cruel and haughty lover. Calidore defeats the lover and forces him to marry Briana without any
dowry. Thus he both puts an end to the custom and earns
the gratitude of the lady. Next Tristram, a youth of royal
birth who has grown up untutored in the woods, kills a
knight who was maltreating his own lady. When reproved
by Calidore for killing a knight when he himself was not
of knightly rank or even a squire, he justifies himself as
an avenger of cruelty and receives the rank of squire at
Calidore's hands.

In the middle of Canto 3 we come to one of the two
main plots, the story of Calepine and Serena. This is tied in
with the story of Calidore and the Beast by the incident
which initiates it. Calidore has the embarrassing misfor-
tune to interrupt the intimate conversation of the two
lovers in a secluded spot in the woods. While he is making
the best of it with courteous apologies, the Blatant Beast
comes rushing past and carries off Serena, giving her some
grievous wounds. Calidore forces the Beast to drop Serena
and continues to pursue it, for it will not stay to fight.
Calepine assists his wounded lady as far as a river, where
he attempts to gain help from Sir Turpine, who mocks at
him and rides off across the ford. Having at length struggled across himself, carrying his lady, Calepine begs for
shelter for her in Turpine's castle. Refused again, they are
obliged to spend the night in the open. The next day, as
Calepine is going slowly on foot, trying to hold Serena on

his horse's back, Turpine gallops up and attacks him. From this plight he is finally rescued by a savage man, whose skin has luckily been rendered invulnerable by some magic means which Spenser promises to explain later on. The savage man not only drives away Turpine but also manages to cure Calepine's wounds with herbs. Serena's wounds he is unable to cure, for they are infested with poison from the bite of the Blatant Beast. While Calepine is waiting in hope of Serena's improvement, he sees a bear carrying off a human infant in its mouth. Giving chase, he at length succeeds in rescuing the baby but finds that he has lost his way in the woods. Thus, Serena, first deserted by Calidore, is now bereft of Calepine also.

At this point Arthur and Timias come into the picture. It seems that Timias, while separated from Arthur, had been bitten by the Blatant Beast and is still suffering from the wound. Arthur conducts him and Serena, fellow-victims of the Beast, to an old hermit to be cured. This hermit was formerly a brave and active knight, whose long career had made him well acquainted with the ways of the world. Failing in his attempts to cure his patients by medicine, he applies his knowledge of psychology and tells them that the cause of their trouble is mental and spiritual rather than physical. Paralleling the treatment given Red Cross at the House of Holiness, he urges them to restrain their wills, subdue their desires, bridle loose delights, shun secrecy, and talk in open sight. The meaning of all this is that the bite of the Beast signifies damage to one's reputation. Serena has suffered from her lack of discretion in making a secret rendezvous with her lover in the woods. Timias, we remember, had suffered the loss of Belphoebe's esteem in Book IV through his too great tenderness to Amoret while rescuing her. The whole Timias-Belphoebe story concerns the relations of Sir Walter Raleigh with the queen and his loss of favor with her through his secret love affair and eventual marriage with Elizabeth Throgmorton. The extreme importance given to the preservation of one's reputation, which may seem too much to an age of greatly relaxed social regulations, is best interpreted by thinking of its importance at the royal court where everything depended upon what the queen thought of a person.

The hermit's cure of Serena by his insight into her character and past actions concludes the moral and allegorical part of her adventures. There follows the highly exciting story of her capture by the savages and subsequent rescue by Calepine, which seems to have been put in to provide a dramatic reunion of the lovers. As she and Timias are riding along, they meet a beautiful lady being led on a horse by a villain named Disdain, while from behind she is scourged by another villain named Scorn. Timias tries to rescue her but is overcome himself by Disdain's iron club. When Serena is thus deprived of her protector, she flies away to avoid capture herself. Exhausted at last by her efforts, she falls asleep on a grassy spot deep in the woods. Here she is discovered by a tribe of cannibals, whose satisfaction at finding such a toothsome morsel is described by Spenser with great gusto:

Canto VIII
37-39

> Soone as they spied her, Lord, what gladfull glee
> They made amongst themselves; but when her face
> Like the faire ivory shining they did see,
> Each gan his fellow solace and embrace.
> For joy of such good hap by heavenly grace
> Whether to slay her there upon the place,
> Or suffer her out of her sleepe to wake,
> And then eat her at once; or many meals to make.

The best advisement was of bad, to let her
Sleep out her fill, without encomberment:
For sleep they said would make her battill better.
Then when she wakt, they all gave one consent,
Since by the grace of God she there was sent,
Unto their God they would her sacrifize,
Whose share, her guiltlesse bloud they would present,
But of her dainty flesh they did devize
To make a common feast, and feed with gourmandize.

So round about her they themselves did place
Upon the grasse,.and diversely dispose,
As each thought best to spend the lingering space.
Some with their eyes the daintest morsels chose;
Some praise her paps, some praise her lips and nose;
Some whet their knives and strip their elbows bare:
The priest himselfe a garland doth compose
Of finest flowres, and with full busie care
His bloody vessels wash and holy fire prepare.

When she awakes, a scene of barbaric activity takes place.
The savages press around her, whooping and hallooing
and stripping her of her jewels and of every stitch of clothing. The exposure of her beauties inflames many of the
savages with lust, but they are sternly repressed by the
priest, who says that she is dedicated to their god. In the
meantime darkness has come on. Lit only by the sacrificial
fire, the wild rabble crowds around the altar where the
priest is about to slay the naked girl, while bagpipes and
horns fill the air with weird and terrible music.

This scene is the build-up for Calepine's last-minute
rescue of his lady, whom he has long sought. Coming by
chance through that part of the woods, he is attracted by
the noise and the flames:

There by th' uncertaine glims of starry night,
And by the twinkling of their sacred fire,
He mote perceive a little dawning sight

Of all, which there was doing in that quire:
Mongst whom a woman spoyld of all attire
He spied, lamenting her unluckie strife,
And groning sore from grieved hart entire,
Eftsoones he saw one with a naked knife
Ready to launch her breast, and let out loved life.

This sudden flash of the same scene as viewed by an approaching rescuer is a masterpiece of descriptive art and narrative suspense. Wielding his sword right and left among the intervening throng, Calepine reaches the altar just in time to stop the descending blow. The frightened savages disperse, leaving him to care for the lady. He has no clothes with which to cover her, and her own embarrassment makes her keep her back turned to him and refuse to talk. In the uncertain light, for the fire has died down, the lovers do not recognize one another. They and the expectant reader must await the interesting recognition scene which will take place at sunrise. But like the pursuing lover on Keats's Grecian urn, Calepine is doomed to postpone perpetually the mingled joy and embarrassment of discovering his own Serena in the disrobed unfortunate whom he has rescued. In postponing this event for future treatment Spenser allowed the shears of the fates to cut off a scene which would have called forth all his powers of psychological intuition, but at least he left these two lovers reunited in fact, even though not in their own knowledge, instead of wandering hopelessly in search of each other like Amoret and Scudamour.

Skipping over Arthur's punishment of the cruel and traitorous Turpine and his rescue of Timias from the giant Disdain, we return to Calidore. When he forced the Blatant Beast to drop the wounded Serena, he hoped also to capture the Beast. This, however, he was unable to do because the Beast feared him and fled with incredible speed. Continuing to follow it, Calidore came at length upon a little community of shepherds. These simple folk are unable to give him any information about the object of his search, but their courteous entertainment is so kindly that he is easily persuaded to rest himself awhile. Among them he finds the fair Pastorella, a beautiful girl who is reputed to be the daughter of an old courtier, now retired to country life, named Melibee. This wise old man discourses on the advantages of a contented simple life over the distracting and disappointing rivalries of the court. Calidore listens with growing interest and finally expresses a wish that his lot were cast in such a carefree state. Melibee replies that men do not always know what is best for them and should not blame fortune, since it is the mind that makes good or ill and a man's happiness is in his own hands. The result of this conversation is that Calidore decides to remain among the shepherds while he considers what he shall do about his own future. Spenser makes it clear that this abandonment of his quest and indecision about himself are as much connected with Pastorella as they are with her father's views on retirement. Calidore, in fact, becomes her declared suitor and endeavors in every way to please her. He finds that his compliments and court manners, to which she is unused, do not move her at all, so he becomes a shepherd and goes out in the fields to help her with her work. Poor Coridon, his rustic rival for her affections, now has little chance against Calidore, who being courtesy itself is able to adjust his manners to his new station with complete success. The course of true love this time runs smooth. At the end of Canto 9 Calidore becomes the accepted lover of Pastorella.

Spenser crowns this idyll of pastoral love with a vision

of the Graces as the patrons of courtesy and also as patrons of himself as a pastoral poet. Wandering in the woods one day, Calidore finds himself in a grassy amphitheater surrounded with trees. In this clearing, the description of which suggests the natural and climatic charms of the Bower of Bliss without any of the latter's artificial hothouse quality, Colin Clout is piping for "an hundred naked maidens lilly white, all raunged in a ring and dauncing in delight." In the center are the three Graces doing honor to another damsel placed like a precious gem in its setting.

> Those were the Graces, daughters of delight,
> Handmaides of Venus, which are wont to haunt
> Upon this hill, and daunce there day and night:
> Those three to men all gifts of grace do graunt,
> And all that Venus in herself doth vaunt
> Is borrowed of them. But that faire one,
> That in the midst was placed paravaunt,
> Was she to whom that shepherd piped alone,
> That made him pipe so merrily as never none.
>
> She was to weete that jolly shepherd's lasse,
> Which piped there unto that merry rout,
> That jolly shepherd which there piped was
> Poore Colin Clout (who knows not Colin Clout?)
> He piped apace, whilest they him daunst about.
> Pipe, jolly shepherd, pipe thou now apace
> Unto thy love, that made thee low to lout:
> Thy love is present there with thee in place,
> Thy love is there advaunst to be another Grace.

Thus does the poet insert himself and the lady of his adoration into one of the great passages of his poem. The passage must have been written near the period of his marriage to Elizabeth Boyle and his ecstatic *Epithalamion* upon it. In writing of the successful courtship of Calidore he was

obviously moved to link with it for all future ages the
wonder and the mystery of his own love.

This scene, nevertheless, was not put in simply to celebrate Spenser's private joy. Like the vision of the New
Jerusalem near the end of Book I, it is meant to give a
flash of insight into the very source of the virtue to which
the book is devoted. The explanation is fittingly put into
the mouth of Colin himself:

> These three on men all gracious gifts bestow,
> Which decke the body or adorne the minde,
> To make them lovely or well favored show,
> As comely carriage, entertainement kind,
> Sweet semblaunt, friendly offices that binde,
> And all the complements of curtesie:
> They teach us how to each degree and kind
> We should ourselves demeane, to low, to high,
> To friends, to foes, which skill men call civility.
>
> Therefore they always smoothly seem to smile,
> That we likewise should mylde and gentle be,
> And also naked are, that without guile
> Or false dissemblaunce all them plaine may see,
> Simple and true, from covert malice free;
> And eke themselves so in their daunce they bore,
> That two of them still froward seem'd to bee,
> But one still towards shew'd herself afore;
> That good should from us goe, than come in greater store.

Never did Spenser produce a better illustration of his con-
tention in the letter to Sir Walter Raleigh that doctrine is
"more profitable and gratious by ensample than by rule."
This little summary of the physical and moral elements of
courtesy would have been mere didacticism if spoken by
Melibee or the old hermit; but after the breath-taking surprise of shapely white limbs moving in graceful dance
against a background of stately shade trees it comes to
Calidore and to the reader with emotional conviction

rather than intellectual assent. One realizes more fully, for instance, the importance of physical grace in courtesy. Kindness, generosity, friendly offices, may be attained by all who love their neighbors as themselves, but there is an accompanying "sweet semblaunt" and "comely carriage" which seems to be the gift of nature alone and which confers a crowning grace upon those who are fortunate enough to have it.

C. S. Lewis, whom we have had occasion to cite before, has called attention to the significant contrast between this scene and the Bower of Bliss in Book II. Both scenes are endowed with great beauty, but that of the Bower is artificial while this is in the midst of unspoiled nature. Both scenes have naked ladies prominently featured in them. In the Bower of Bliss none of these ladies is doing anything commendable, whereas the hundred naked maidens of Book VI are engaged in the creation of an artistic form, the dance. When the bathing girls discover Guyon, they shamelessly tempt him; when Calidore finally makes himself known on that woodland green, the dance dissolves and only Colin is left. Remembrance of the Bower of Bliss on Guyon's part would have led only to useless speculation on what would have happened if the palmer had not been with him, but Calidore's memory of the naked Graces is an inspiration to the practice of true courtesy.

Following the disappearance of the dancers and Colin's explanation of them comes a sudden break-up of Calidore's pastoral paradise. During his absence a band of brigands, whose stronghold was on an island, raids the home of the shepherds and carries off Pastorella and her friends. The pirate captain, having fallen in love with Pastorella, tries to keep her for himself when the rest of the captives are sold to slave traders. His action precipitates civil war among his followers, during which Coridon escapes. He finds Calidore desperately searching for Pastorella and tells him where to find her. Concealing his weapons under his shepherd's cloak, Calidore gets into the island hideout and rescues her. Since Melibee and the other shepherds have been killed in the brawl, he takes her to the nearest castle. In this romantic narrative the reader is not surprised to learn that she is the long-lost daughter of the lord and lady of this castle.

During all the pastoral interlude the Blatant Beast has been wrecking monasteries, wounding the clergy, and robbing churches. Calidore now returns to the quest. Driving the Beast into a narrow place, like a rat in a corner, he captures him and ties him up with a muzzle and a chain. And so for a time slander ceased in fairyland. Yet the book ends with a warning that each age must subdue him for itself. Whether through wicked fate or fault or men, he eventually breaks his chain and gets free:

> So now he raungeth through the world againe,
> And rageth sore in each degree and state;
> Ne any is, that may him now restraine,
> He growen is so great and strong of late,
> Barking and biting all that doe him bate,
> Albe they worthy blame, or cleare of crime:
> Ne spareth he most learned wits to rate,
> Ne spareth he the gentle poet's rime,
> But rends without regard of person or of time.

In the treatment of courtesy as a virtue Spenser faced a problem which did not arise in the other five books. The other virtues belonged to mankind in general, but the Renaissance tradition regarded courtesy as being the special possession of royal courts and noble households. In this tradition Spenser grew up, and to it his writings always outwardly conform. Nevertheless it is hard for anyone who reads his works attentively to believe that in mature life he continued to believe that courts in his day were really the home of true courtesy as he conceived it. On several occasions he nobly praised the best type of courtier, but these passages are outweighed by the biting attacks on court life found elsewhere. In "Mother Hubberd's Tale" and *Colin Clout's Come Home Again* we find the praise and the blame both occurring in each poem. The praise, though nobly expressed, sounds conventional, but the blame has the ring of bitter personal conviction. Similarly in Book VI we find in the prologue and in the opening stanza of the first canto the expected praise of court manners, while in the ninth canto Melibee and Calidore agree in preferring simple country life to the vanity and mercenary ambitions of the capital. If courts are the fountainheads of courtesy, we should expect to find scenes in which Calidore, or perhaps Arthur, is present in a royal palace, some parallel to the court of Mercilla in Book V. Instead of this we find that no book in the *Faerie Queene* so persistently avoids courts and castles. Instead of glorifying courtesy in the halls of princes, Spenser glorifies it in the woods. And to show that this is no mistake or oversight, he introduces himself as Colin Clout, the simple shepherds' poet, being favored by the three Graces.

It is clear, then, that the pastoral interlude is not merely a pretty Arcadian idyll, a dereliction from duty put in because Spenser enjoyed it. On the contrary, I think it represents Spenser's final rejection of political ambition and his defense of his retired life as an Irish planter. Already in *Colin Clout's Come Home Again*, written between 1591 and 1595, he had shown his pleasure in the Irish scenery around his new home, and in the surviving cantos of Book VII he places the great council of the gods on the top of a mountain near Kilcolman. The writing of Book VI took place during the happiest years of Spenser's life. It is only natural that he should think of London as the place where glory and reputation were to be had but where troubles, delays, and envious opposition beset every ambitious man. We are not told what Calidore did after the Blatant Beast was safely chained up, but there is no indication that he had any desire to continue at court. I suspect that he went back to see what had become of Pastorella's sheep.

If Spenser did not really believe that courtesy lived only in courts, where did he think it was found? The conclusion to be drawn from Book VI is that it comes from noble or gentle birth. Again the pastoral interlude is instructive. Melibee, a former courtier, possesses courtesy; so does Pastorella, who later turns out to be the daughter of a knight; Calidore remains a model of courtesy even when following rustic occupations in borrowed clothing. On the other hand, no shepherd except Colin Clout, the divinely inspired poet, is represented as notably courteous, and Coridon is held up to ridicule as a boorish lout and a coward. The examples of Tristram and the savage man are equally instructive. Tristram's courtesy is obviously attributable to his royal birth, even though he has grown up in the woods. The savage man, whose faithful care of Serena is so highly commended, is of mysterious origin, but Spenser specifically states "certes he was borne of noble blood" and promises to tell us the story later. We can be certain that Spencer means to say in this book that courtesy in its full flower, as opposed to simple kindness or humanity, is found only in those of gentle birth. Just what this term implies we cannot be sure. In the *Faerie Queene* it seems to mean that one must be of knightly family, although Satyrane, a highly courteous man, is the illegitimate son of a lady and a satyr; in Elizabethan life it probably meant that one must be a "gentleman." Nowhere in Spenser do we find the opinion expressed in Chaucer's *Gentilesse* that courtesy or gentility is a gift of God which may crop up in any person—even in the lowly Griselda.

If Spenser's conception of courtesy is not a democratic one, which indeed we could hardly expect it to be in his age and environment, it is at least a nobly broad and humane conception. It begins with the heart and extends to cover even grace of bodily movement. "The gentle minde by gentle deedes is knowne," Spenser tells us, quoting Chaucer. And again, "The gentle hart itselfe bewrayes in doing gentle deedes with frank delight." Courtesy is not an imposed discipline; it is the outward expression of an inner delight in gentle deeds. It surpasses justice because it adds love to law; and so it is not surprising to find that Calidore is more likable than Arthegal. Because courtesy springs from affection, it is not fastidious. "Entire affection hateth nicer hands," Spenser wrote in Book I in regard to Arthur, the personification of all the virtues, and in Book VI he makes Calidore reprove the young lady who was too dainty to carry her bloody, wounded lover upon her back. A courteous person has true dignity exactly because he never thinks of his own dignity. A courteous person is also without guile and free from malice and slander. It is here that the pursuit of the Blatant Beast fits in. Courtesy abounds in friendly offices and kind entertainment, done not as a duty but because the gentle heart delights in such things. It is the embodiment of the spirit of love defined by Paul in his First Epistle to the Corinthians. To these moral and social qualities Spenser adds sweetness of expression and grace of movement: "comely carriage" and "sweet semblaunt." Although partially attainable by voluntary practice, these endowments are essentially the gift of nature and of the Graces, who are themselves the ideal expression of comeliness:

Thereto great helpe Dame Nature selfe doth lend:
For some so goodly gratious are by kind,
That every action doth them much commend,
And in the eyes of men great liking find;
Which others, that have greater skill in mind,
Though they enforce themselves, cannot attaine.
For everie thing, to which one is inclined,
Doth best become, and greatest grace doth gaine:
Yet praise likewise deserve good thewes, enforst with paine.

Because of the imperfection of human nature this gift sometimes falls upon an unworthy person. Blandina, in Canto 6, is described as possessing the outward graces of courtesy to a high degree, yet her whole demeanor was only a trap "to some hid end to make more easy way."

Spenser would not have been an Elizabethan if he had not made order and degree an important part of courtesy. Colin Clout explains to Calidore that the Graces

teach us how to each degree and kind
We should ourselves demeane, to low, to high,
To friends, to foes, which skill men call civility.

And at the beginning of Canto 2 Spenser had already stated that this knowledge of the proper behavior toward degrees and categories of people is very important for both knights and ladies. To the Renaissance mind this did not mean haughty aristocratic condescension toward the lower classes. Such behavior they saw as a fault and attributed it to the *nouveaux riches* as a class characteristic. Respect for order and degree, on the other hand, was respect for God's organization of the universe. They thought of both animate and inanimate nature as great hierarchies in which order and degree were implicit and eternal. God was above the angels, and the angels were above men, while men were above the animals. Similarly, within the human race the king was above the ruling class, and the ruling class (whose duty it was to rule, not to be idle) was above the yeomen and craftsmen. There was no theory that the nobleman was a better *man* than the yeoman, but his position was higher in the order of society. A man could, however, forfeit the respect due to his position if he failed to live up to its requirements. Although it was against the law of chivalry for a common man to presume to attack a knight, Calidore commends Tristram, of whose royal birth he is unaware, for killing a knight who had been guilty of cruelty toward a lady. In another instance we find the cruelty of Disdain and Scorn toward Mirabella approved because this time it was the lady who had abused the privileges of her position.

Calidore himself is a model of courteous behavior in many different circumstances. His bearing toward enemies is shown first and then his bearing toward social equals in need of help. His treatment of Tristram, inferior in rank but equal in birth, is nicely differentiated from his treatment of Coridon, a well-meaning but boorish rustic. The whole episode of his stay among the shepherds shows his ability to put off entirely for a time his superior social rank and enter into the life of a country community as an equal. His conversations with Melibee show his deference toward a man who is his superior in age and experience even though not in social rank.

The whole of Book VI is a plea for, and a praise of, good will among men. It keeps before us the idea that the proper training of the emotions is the essential thing. We must not merely learn to do gentle, kindly, and humane things because they are right and profitable for society; we must take delight in doing them. Britomart, at the end of Book III, did not risk the peril of Busyrane's curtain of fire because of duty to society but because of an instant welling-up in her heart of love for a fellow human being in trouble. Calidore would have done the same thing. Tristram and the savage man have grown up without proper instruction in social duties, but within them is the gentle heart, the source of all courtesy, and they act spontaneously through love. Courtesy in Spenser's hands comes very close to being the virtue which embraces all the rest. Holiness, temperance, chaste love, friendship, and justice all have a place in it. What other six virtues were to come in the unwritten portion of the poem we do not know, although the publisher of the 1609 edition said that constancy was to be one, but the legend of Sir Calidore is a very fitting close to the part we have.

CHAPTER VII

MUTABILITY

IN 1609, ten years after Spenser's death, the publisher Matthew Lownes brought out an edition of the *Faerie Queene* in which there appeared a previously unpublished fragment entitled "Two Cantos of Mutabilitie: Which, both for Forme and Matter, appear to be parcell of some following Booke of the *Faerie Queene*, under the legend of *Constancie*." Although no one has ever discovered where Lownes got this new material, there can be no doubt that his statement is correct. The verse form is the stanza which Spenser used only for the *Faerie Queene*, and there are two unmistakable references linking it to that poem. Whether the title of "Constancie" was in the manuscript or was a guess on the part of the publisher is open to question. Editors have numbered the book as VII, for convenience, but the numbering of the cantos themselves as 6 and 7 (and two stanzas of 8) could have originated only with the author himself.

The subject of mutability was one which had been in Spenser's mind for many years. As a schoolboy he had translated a series of poems from Petrarch and Du Bellay for Van der Noodt's *Theatre for Worldlings*, all of them stressing changes of fortune or falls from high estate. In 1591 he had published a number of poems on similar themes in his own *Complaints*. Of these the "Ruins of Rome" and the "Ruins of Time" may serve as examples. The former, which is a translation from Du Bellay, contrasts the ancient power and glory of Rome with the pres-

ent decay of its temples and palaces. The third stanza gives
the theme of the whole poem:

> Thou stranger, which for Rome in Rome here seekest,
> And nought of Rome in Rome perceiv'st at all,
> These same old walls, old arches, which thou seest,
> Old palaces, is that which Rome men call.
> Behold what wreake, what ruin, and what waste,
> And how that she, which with her mighty powre
> Tam'd all the world, hath tam'd herselfe at last,
> The pray of Time, which all things doth devowre.
> Rome now of Rome is th'onely funerall,
> And onely Rome of Rome hath victorie;
> Ne ought save Tyber hastening to his fall
> Remains of all: O world's inconstancie!
> > That which is firm doth flit and fall away,
> > And that is flitting which doth abide and stay.

The "Ruins of Time" starts off in a similar vein with the
spirit of the deserted city of Verulam bewailing the loss of
its departed glory. Then it shifts to a poetic necrology of
the Dudley family, in which Spenser laments the deaths
of the earls of Warwick and of Leicester and of their
nephew Sir Philip Sidney. Here we have the decay of men
and their fame linked with the decay of institutions and
buildings. Neither of these themes was in any way original
with Spenser. One he derived from Du Bellay, and the
other goes back through the *Mirror for Magistrates* to Lyd-
gate and Boccaccio, to carry the ancestry no further. The
deaths of both his early patrons, Leicester and Sidney, had
brought the insecurity of man's state sharply to Spenser's
attention on his return to England in 1589.

In the *Faerie Queene*, exclusive of the fragment of Book
VII, we find a number of comments on the mutability of
this world. First, there are those passages which are concerned with the chances and changes of mortal life—fail-

ures, accidents, diseases, war, death. This is mutability
as it affects the lives of individuals. It causes not only personal tragedies but also doubts and questionings as to the
purposes of God. Arthur speaks of this in Canto 9 of the
first book:

> Full hard it is (quoth he) to read aright
> The course of heavenly cause, or understand
> The secret meaning of the eternall might,
> That rules men's ways and rules the thoughts of living wight.

Second, there is the idea of the progressive deterioration
of the world and man. Looking either in the Bible or in the
ancient classics, men of the Renaissance found descrip-
tions of a primitive age of purity and innocence followed
by the rise of sin and progressive moral degeneration.
Both theologians and scientists agreed that physical nature
had suffered change and decay. This is a favorite thought
with Spenser. The moral faults of his own age disturbed
him, and he liked to contrast them with the virtue of what
he calls "the antique age." Characteristic passages of this
sort are found in the eighth canto of Book IV and in the
fifth stanza of the prologue to Book VI. The most complete statement of the deterioration of the world, both
moral and physical, is in the prologue to Book V:

> So oft as I with state of present time
> The image of the antique world compare,
> When as man's age was in his freshest prime
> And the first blossom of faire vertue bare,
> Such odds I find twixt those, and these which are,
> As that, through long continuance of his course,
> Me seemes the world is runne quite out of square
> From the first point of his appointed source,
> And being once amiss growes daily worse and worse.
>
> For from the golden age that first was named,
> It's now at earst become a stonie one;

Mutability

And men themselves, the which at first were framed
Of earthly mould, and formed of flesh and bone,
Are now transformed into hardest stone:
Such as behind their backs (so backward bred)
Were throwne by Pyrrha and Deucalione:
And if than those may any worse be red,
They into that ere long will be degenered.

So much for mankind and his lower world. But the heavens
too, which some thought pure and changeless, give evidence of change from their original state:

For who so list into the heavens looke
And search the courses of the rowling spheres
Shall find that from the point where they first tooke
Their setting forth, in these few thousand years
They all are wandred much; that plaine appears.
For that same fleecy Ram, which bore
Phrixus and Helle from their stepdame's feares,
Hath now forgot where he was placed of yore,
And shouldered hath the Bull which fayre Europa bore.

And eke the Bull hath with his bow-bent horne
So hardly butted those two twinnes of Jove
That they have crushed the crab, and quite him borne
Into the great Nemean lion's grove.
So now all range, and do at random rove
Out of their proper places far away,
And all this world with them amisse doe move,
And all his creatures from their course astray,
Till they arrive at their last ruinous decay.

Spenser goes on to say that, among the planets, Mars,
Saturn, and the sun (then counted as a planet) have shifted
from their original courses, if the Egyptian astronomers
are to be trusted.

Another aspect of mutability is the changeable appearances of persons and things according to our knowledge or
ignorance of their true nature. No one, I think, can read

through the *Faerie Queene* without being struck by Spenser's prominent use of this theme of deception. Not only does he remark upon the false appearances of things in didactic passages, but he also bases a number of important plot developments upon the dangers and mistakes caused by failure to recognize them. The first piece of important action in Book I is the deceiving of the hero by supernatural means. Later he is again deceived, with more disastrous results but by more natural means. Duessa, an old hand at seductions, he believes to be a pure and innocent maiden in distress; the court of Lucifera he believes to be the true embodiment of chivalric honor until he is enlightened by the discoveries of his dwarf. Archimago, who first appears as a false hermit, turns out to be the very spirit of deception. He even unintentionally deceives his own colleagues and gets well beaten up before the mistakes are rectified. Through Books III–V there runs the parallel pair of characters, Florimel and false Florimel. The latter has been so ingeniously constructed by a witch that she deceives everyone who meets her until she is finally confronted by the true Flormel. Spenser emphasizes the universal success of this false flirt by making her win the beauty contest at Satyrane's tournament. Braggadochio passes for a real knight, though he is none, for a long time before he is exposed by Arthegal at Florimel's wedding. Finally there is Blandina, who illustrates Spenser's claim in the prologue to Book VI that false courtesy, if clever enough, can blind the wisest sight. Blandina gives every outward appearance of courtesy, graciousness, and a mind solicitous for the welfare of others, yet it is all put on. She is accustomed to lure people into a trap by these means entirely for her own ends, and she is able to deceive no less a person than Arthur himself.

Mutability

It is interesting to consider why these deceptive characters succeed so long at the expense of the virtuous ones.
Duessa and false Florimel depend almost entirely upon sex
appeal. Their beauty and their claim upon male protective-
ness do the trick. The victory of false Florimel in the
beauty contest, where she has aroused the admiration of
all the knights, indicates that Spenser thought that everyone falls into error who judges beauty only by external
appearance. Yet we must remember that Arthur's judgment of Blandina, which is based on behavior rather than
on a pretty face, is no more reliable. Archimago also, to
take a male example, succeeds remarkably well in his numerous disguises, although the results achieved often seem
negligible. The virtuous always are at a disadvantage in
dealing with the deceivers, for their normal reaction to
other people is one of trust and respect. It is evident, too,
that there are some kinds of deceit, such as Blandina's, for
instance, which are impossible to detect until it is too
late.

Why was Spenser so much concerned with the theme of
deception? There may, of course, have been experiences
in his private life which lay behind this concern, but we
can find other reasons by looking at his artistic methods
and at the history of Elizabethan England. The element of
disguise was playing a large part in the political and spiritual warfare between the British government (the church
was part of the government) and the Roman church. On
one side, Elizabeth had been excommunicated by the pope
and, on the other, Catholic priests had been forbidden to
enter England. As a result of this order many Jesuits came
into the country in disguise to minister to English Catho-
lics and to make converts. They were accused also of
plotting against the queen's life. Consequently every Eng-

lishman who kept well informed on current news and rumors had a lively interest in the proposition that people are not always what they seem. It is this religio-political connotation of deception which is most stressed in Book I, where Archimago and Duessa are clearly labeled as Roman agents. In the rest of the *Faerie Queene* the explanation is less specific and more concerned with Spenser's own frame of mind and outlook on life. Spenser was an idealist who would have liked nothing better than to believe that truth is beauty, beauty truth, as his own "Hymn of Beauty" shows; but he was troubled with a stubbornly realistic respect for what he observed in life as it is. Everything ought to be quite simple. We ought to desire the good when we see it and detest the bad. Unfortunately, in the imperfect state of humanity, our reason does not always distinguish clearly and our foresight does not remind us that what seems a present good may soon become a future evil. Nothing was clearer to Spenser, if we may judge from the *Faerie Queene*, than the reality of temptations to evil and the difficulty of recognizing them clearly when they come. A considerable degree of intelligence was required as well as a well-developed moral sense, and not enough of the virtuous people in life possessed this intelligence. The higher the goal, the more fatal are the dangers involved. In the books of holiness and justice the heroes both suffer ignominious defeat and have to be rescued by the faithful love of their ladies. This, I believe, is Spenser's answer to the problem. Life is full of deceptions, some harmless and some dangerous even to the most virtuous men. The only remedy is faithful love. Such love in our hearts will preserve us from many evils—in the poem it preserves Britomart from all evils—and from others the love of our fellow-men or the love of God will rescue us.

Finally there is the conception of mutability as the basis

of God's order for this world. Just as the various positions in an intricate dance might seem aimless if viewed apart from the whole design, so is all partial evil universal good. Change and chance are part of God's purpose for us now, but in the New Jerusalem at the end of the world all will be peace and changeless order. This is the theme of the "Two Cantos of Mutability." Before turning to these cantos, however, we must consider an interesting and important passage in the description of the Garden of Adonis in Book III (Canto 6). In this garden are the seeds of all living things. Their matter is indestructible, but their form is subject to time and decay. Time, therefore, is the great enemy of the Garden of Adonis. To overcome this inescapable mortality, there is constant rebirth. Substance returns to the Garden again and again to receive new form. Presiding over this process are Venus and Adonis, the symbols of fertility:

> There wont faire Venus often to enjoy
> Her deare Adonis' joyous company
> And reap sweet pleasure of the wanton boy:
> There yet, some say, in secret he does ly,
> Lapped in flowres and pretious spicery,
> By her hid from the world, and from the skill
> Of Stygian gods, which doe her love envy;
> But she herself, whenever that she will,
> Possesseth him, and of his sweetness takes her fill.

> And sooth it seemes they say: for he may not
> For ever die, and ever buried bee
> In balefull night, where all things are forgot;
> All be he subject to mortalitie,
> Yet is eterne in mutabilitie,
> And by succession made perpetuall,
> Transformed oft, and chaunged diverslie:
> For him the father of all formes they call;
> Therefore needs mote he live, that living gives to all.

Creative love, Spenser says, is eternal; but its expression, subject to the changes of time, is "transformed oft and chaunged diverslie."

The "Mutability Cantos" are an elaboration of this theme. Mutability is a Titaness who seeks to overthrow Jove's rule and regain the lost power of her line. Already she has corrupted the earth and mankind. As an opening attack upon the gods she pushes her way into the palace of the moon-goddess Cynthia:

> Her sitting on an ivory throne shee found,
> Drawne of two steeds, th'one black, the other white,
> Environd with tenne thousand stars around,
> That duly her attended day and night;
> And by her side there ran her page, that hight
> Vesper, whom we the evening starre intend:
> That with his torche, still twinkling like twylight,
> Her lightened all the way that she should wend,
> And joy to weary wandering travelers did lend.

When she tries to pluck Cynthia from her throne by force, Jove interferes and summons her to a council of the gods in his own palace. Here Mutability presents her claim in no uncertain terms. Jove denies her right but offers to restore her to a place in heaven if she will receive it as a favor from him as her gracious lord and sovereign. Mutability's answer is an appeal to the God of Nature, Jove's superior. He is obliged to grant this appeal, and a time is set for holding the great trial upon Arlo Hill. This is Spenser's poetical name for the highest mountain near Kilcolman, called Galteemore. Mention of it leads him to digress from his narrative with a mythological tale about some of the Irish rivers in the neighborhood, and with this tale the canto comes to an end. The next canto is devoted to the trial. When the gods are all assembled on the broad summit of Arlo, the great goddess Nature appears, veiled and dressed in shining raiment like that of Christ in the Transfiguration. Her characteristics are mystical. She is veiled so that none may see her face. She is ever young, yet full of age.

> Great Nature, ever young yet full of eld,
> Still moving, yet unmoved from her sted;
> Unseen of any, yet of all beheld.

Mutability is sufficiently awed by this majestic presence to speak humbly before the throne, yet she presents her case fully and convincingly. Men, animals, and the physical world are all subject to her already, she says, and she calls forth a great pageant of witnesses to prove it. First come the seasons, then the months, the hours, day and night, and finally life and death, all presented in Spenser's best pictorial style:

> When these were past, thus gan the Titanesse:
> Lo, mighty mother, now be judge and say,
> Whether in all thy creatures more or lesse
> CHANGE doth not raign and bear the greatest sway:
> For who sees not, that Time on all doth pray?
> But times do change and move continually.
> So nothing here long standeth in one stay:
> Wherefore, this lower world who can deny
> But to be subject still to Mutabilitie?

When Jove tries to rebut this argument by saying that the gods rule both time and change, Mutability tells him that the gods themselves are changeable and therefore should be subject to her. Her proof is based on the old identification of the gods with the planets which bear their names. Cynthia, the moon, is the most changeful of all; the sun suffers eclipses; Mercury, Mars, and Saturn have changed their courses. The sum of all her arguments is that there is nothing unchanged in the whole universe. The goddess

Nature considers the evidence in silence for some time, while the whole assembly awaits her decision. This decision, a model of judicial brevity, must be quoted in full:

> I well consider all that ye have said,
> And find that all things stedfastness doe hate
> And changed be: yet being rightly wayd
> They are not changed from their first estate,
> But by their change their being do dilate:
> And turning to themselves at length againe,
> Do work their own perfection so by fate:
> Then over them change doth not rule and raigne,
> But they raigne over change and do their states maintaine.
>
> Cease, therefore, daughter, further to aspire,
> And thee content thus to be ruled by mee:
> For thy decay thou seekst by thy desire;
> But time shall come that all shall changed bee,
> And from thenceforth none no more change shall see.
> So was the Titanesse put downe and whist,
> And Jove confirm'd in his imperiall see.
> Then was that whole assembly quite dismist,
> And Nature's self did vanish, whither no man wist.

This judgment, which at first sight may remind modern readers of the theory of evolution, is not based on any idea of progress toward a goal but rather on one of cyclical change. The end returns to the beginning. But this end is not final; after it will come the Day of Judgment, followed by the new universe which shall be changeless because perfect.

The solution which Spenser puts in Nature's mouth is a courageous attempt to face the facts and at the same time give them an idealistic interpretation. As he looked at his own age, he saw everything seemingly in a state of violent change. The universal church had been split, not just in two, but in half-a-dozen pieces. Even the Anglican church

itself seemed to be constantly shifting its position as tradi-
tionalists and reformers battled for supremacy in its coun-
cils. Politically the scene was equally chaotic. The great
Hapsburg empire was torn with revolt. France seethed
with factional warfare, and a king of France had been
murdered; the queen of Scotland had been deposed by the
Scots and executed by the English. England, after centuries
of male rule, was governed by a woman—a woman whose
fate it had been to be first declared illegitimate by her
father and then reinstated in the succession by that same
father's last will and testament. And after she died, none
could say what would happen. Radicals even talked of a
republic. In the field of science strange theories were being propounded to explain stubborn facts of astronomical
observation. Many intelligent Englishmen were aware of
these theories—Spenser, as a close friend of Raleigh, certainly was—but they did not know what to think of them.
In geography the fascinating new discoveries were bringing into existence a new picture of the world. Here again
Spenser's association with Raleigh put him in the forefront
of knowledge. The *Faerie Queene* is liberally sprinkled
with references to America. All these evidences of change
were accepted by Spenser as irrefutable. Nature does not
challenge a single bit of Mutability's evidence. The problem was to interpret it. Unwilling to be satisfied with a
merely chaotic universe with no plan or purpose, Spenser
adopted the theory which he had used in describing the
functioning of the Garden of Adonis in Book III. Just as
Adonis, the father of all forms, is "eterne in mutabilitie,"
so here the physical world and human institutions are declared to be constantly changing but subject to the eternal
control of a directing power. They work their own per-
fection through their changes.

[167]

Intellectually this explanation satisfied Spenser, but emotionally he was no more calm at the sight of the upheavals of his time than we are today. He would have preferred peace and stability. His reaction to his own picture of great Nature, moving yet unmoved, is like that of the Red Cross Knight seeing the vision of the New Jerusalem after all his trials and defeats. Both would for the moment give up the love of this vain life if they could only be transported to eternal peace:

> When I bethinke me on that speech whyleare
> Of Mutability, and well it way,
> Meseemes that though she all unworthy were
> Of the heav'ns rule, yet very sooth to say,
> In all things else she beares the greatest sway.
> Which makes me loath this state of life so tickle,
> And love of things so vaine to cast away;
> Whose flowring pride, so fading and so fickle,
> Short Time shall soon cut down with his consuming sickle.
>
> Then gin I thinke on that which Nature sayd,
> Of that same time when no more change shall be,
> But stedfast rest of all things firmely stayd
> Upon the pillars of eternity,
> That is contrayr to Mutabilitie:
> For all that moveth doth in change delight.
> But thenceforth all shall rest eternally
> With Him that is the God of Sabbaoth hight:
> O that great Sabbaoth God, graunt me that Sabbaoth's sight.

These are the last published words of Spenser's work. They may even be the last words Spenser ever wrote, although I am inclined myself to date the "Mutability Cantos" near to the prologue of Book V because of the similarity in thought and argument. In any case, they are highly characteristic of Spenser. From beginning to end he saw clearly the defects of society and the tragedies of human life. At the same time, he never failed to set himself courageously to the task of urging upon the readers of his poetry the creation of a better world. The time setting of the *Faerie Queene* is in the remote past, but the faces of the heroes are set resolutely forward. The "gentleman or noble person" whose fashioning is the purpose of the poem is not a static ornamental figure. He is busy creating a better society. Like William Blake, his sword will not sleep in his hand until he has "built Jerusalem in England's green and pleasant land."

Yet Spenser does not threaten or overawe us with an authoritative attitude nor does he sicken us with an easy optimism. No poet was ever less a stuffed shirt. Like his own Red Cross Knight, Spenser has experienced the dangers of the way to the New Jerusalem and knows that they are real. He knows the temptation of the Cave of Despair and the more subtle trial of the Mount of Contemplation, both of them in different ways leading a man to give up the struggle for a better life for mankind. And so, although Spenser makes Nature put Mutability back in her place under Jove, he cannot resist this final cry from the heart. Across the centuries it unites us in spirit with the poet, for it joins our own hopes and fears for a new world about to be born from the strife of nations.

CHAPTER VIII

THE POET OF LOVE

IN SPENSER'S mind the only force capable of overcoming mutability was the power of love. The whole *Faerie Queene* is a continued exposition of this power. As a creative force love between the sexes defeats the ravages of time and death by successively bringing new generations into being; as a redemptive force it heals and repairs the damages in human relations caused by pride, cruelty, and other forms of sin. This belief in the power of love is evident throughout the poem but nowhere more clearly than in the sixth book, where the virtue of courtesy seems to contain within itself all the best qualities of both kinds of love.

To Spenser love was the central force of the universe. Love in the beginning had imposed order and harmony upon the elements; it caused the propagation of men and animals; it impelled men to all noble and virtuous actions; and in the end man was saved by the divine redemptive love of Christ. This conception of love is typical of the Renaissance fusion of classical, medieval, and biblical elements. The basic doctrine of the universality of divine love is Christian, but Spenser, like other poets of his day, used much material from the ancient poets and from the courtly love writers of the Middle Ages in developing his theme. The importance of love in Spenser's work is seen not only in the *Faerie Queene* but also, and quite as strikingly, in his minor poems. I have already discussed in a previous chapter the importance of the love of Colin and Rosalind in the *Shepherds' Calendar*. To this we must add the sonnets, entirely devoted to love, the two wedding odes,

The Poet of Love

Epithalamion and *Prothalamion*, and the *Four Hymns* of earthly and heavenly love and beauty. There are also a few passages of some importance on this theme in *Colin Clout's Come Home Again*.

It will be worth while to think for a moment of the ways in which Spenser has dealt with love in these lesser works. For this purpose the subject may be divided into three parts: courtship, marriage, and the philosophy of love. In treating courtship Spenser is following in the tradition of the medieval romances and their system of courtly love. In the *Shepherds' Calendar* Colin is suffering from an unsuccessful love for Rosalind. Nevertheless we are told in the October eclogue that love has been an ennobling experience for him and has inspired his best poetry. In the sonnets (*Amoretti*) Spenser was necessarily writing in the Petrarchan tradition. This meant that it was customary for the lady to reject the lover's suit. Consequently there are many sonnets describing this state of affairs and much discussion of the lady's pride. The poet regards himself as far below her in worth and defends her pride as commendable self-respect. Another important theme in these sonnets, which comes from Spenser's interest in Neo-Platonic philosophy, is his emphasis on the spiritual side of love. Beauty is of divine origin and leads one to heavenly contemplation. Although his lady is beautiful, her mind "adornd with vertues manifold" is fairer still. And one of his best sonnets, written for Easter Day, unites divine and human love:

> And that thy love we weighing worthily
> May likewise love thee for the same againe:
> And for thy sake that all lyke deare didst buy,
> With love may one another entertayne.
> So let us love, deare love, lyke as we ought,
> Love is the lesson which the Lord us taught.

The Petrarchan attitude is also maintained in *Colin Clout's Come Home Again*, written about the same time as the sonnets. Here Colin says that he is vassal to a lady of peerless beauty and virtue who is high above him and will not grant his suit. In the sonnets, however, this attitude changes in the middle of the sequence. We find that the poet has been accepted by his lady, whose proud heart has been softened by love. The last four sonnets speak of slander and separation but in so vague a way that the reader cannot tell what the poet's situation is supposed to be.

In so far as we may identify Spenser himself with the conventionalized lover of the sonnets this confusion is cleared up by the *Epithalamion* which was published in the same volume. In this poem Spenser describes his own wedding day with considerable local detail. He gives the date as St. Barnabas' Day, the longest of the year; he says that his bride is living near the sea, that she is in a town where there are merchants' daughters; he asks the nymphs and dryads of the rivers and mountains near Kilcolman to wait upon her; and with delightful humor he refers to the croaking of the frogs in the little lake below Kilcolman castle. In one way this completely personal poem, which eschews all dependence upon the poetical fiction of Colin Clout and Rosalind, is quite different from Spenser's other work. In its expression of his own feelings and in its comparative realism it is the most modern of his works. Seen in another way, it is the culmination of his love poetry. In it he triumphantly frees himself from the convention of the proud lady and the humble, languishing lover. The *Epithalamion* shows not only ardent love between the bride and groom but also complete trust and equality. There is not the slightest hint in it that the lady is going to the altar with a condescending attitude or that the poet is offering up humble and unmanly thanks for a boon which she is bestowing upon him. On the other hand, there is no diminution in the poet's belief in the heavenly virtues of her mind. Just as in Sonnet 15 he had climaxed a description of her beauty with a statement that her mind was fairer still, so here after the conventional praise of the bride's bodily attractions he goes on with the following stanzas:

> But if ye saw that which no eyes can see,
> The inward beauty of her lively spright,
> Garnisht with heavenly gifts of high degree,
> Much more then would ye wonder at that sight,
> And stand astonisht lyke to those which red
> Medusa's mazeful head.
> There dwells sweet love and constant chastity,
> Unspotted faith and comely womanhood,
> Regard of honor and mild modesty.
>
> There vertue raynes as queene in royal throne,
> And giveth lawes alone,
> The which the base affections doe obay,
> And yeeld their services unto her will,
> Ne thought of thing uncomely ever may
> Thereto approach to tempt her mind to ill.
> Had ye once seene these her celestial treasures,
> And unrevealed pleasures,
> Then would ye wonder and her praises sing,
> That al the woods should answer and your echo ring.

The erotic element in this wedding ode is much smaller than that in the average Renaissance poem of this sort. Spenser is no prude; he makes us feel the ardent desire of bride and groom for the coming of night and the bridal bed; but this is his own wedding night he is writing about, and he has no intention of running a peepshow for the public. Night and silence come at last. The moonlight begins to flood in through the window, and the poem ends with a prayer for a "large posterity."

Spenser's philosophy of love, so far as the minor works are concerned, is to be found in a passage in *Colin Clout's Come Home Again* and more extensively in the *Four Hymns*. In the former poem (ll. 795–895) Colin explains . to the other shepherds that Love was born before the creation of the world; in fact it was Love who made the world by the power of concord. With beauty as his bait,

> Beautie, the burning lamp of heaven's light,
> Darting her beames into each feeble mind,

he leads men to choose the fairest in their sight for mates. So, he says, Love is lord of all the world by right and rules all creatures by his power. Thus all lovers ought to obey him with chaste hearts. Those outlaws who disobey him and follow base lustfulness do not deserve the name of love. The hymns to Love (Cupid) and Beauty (Venus) do little more than expand these ideas in a series of eloquent stanzas. In the first hymn he emphasizes again the pure and ennobling effect of true love, as opposed to mere lust:

> For love is lord of truth and loialtie,
> Lifting himselfe out of the lowly dust,
> On golden plumes up to the purest skye,
> Above the reach of loathly sinfull lust,
> Whose base affect through cowardly distrust
> Of his weak wings, dare not to heaven fly,
> But like a moldwarp in the earth doth ly.

> His dunghill thoughts, which do themselves enure
> To dirty drosse, no higher dare aspire,
> Ne can his feeble earthly eyes endure
> The flaming light of that celestial fire,
> Which kindleth love in generous desire,
> And makes him mount above the native might
> Of heavie earth, up to the heavens hight.

> Such is the power of that sweet passion,
> That it all sordid basenesse doth expell,

And the refyned mind doth newly fashion
Unto a fairer forme, which now doth dwell
In his high thought, that would itselfe excell;
Which he beholding still with constant sight,
Admires the mirror of so heavenly light.

And in the second hymn he similarly speaks of love as
loyal and true, urging beautiful ladies to give their love
only to such as are likest to themselves in beauty and
virtue, for love is "a celestiall harmony of likely harts."
Beauty, he says in this hymn, is essentially a spiritual quality. It should in turn bring external beauty of appearance
to the body it inhabits, but there are two exceptions to this
rule. First, through "unaptnesse in the substance found,"
the spirit may be unable to mold the body to its desired
beauty. On the other hand, beauty is often abused, so that
those who have the external appearance of beauty are unworthy of it. Thus does Spenser's sturdy realism in observing life keep him from advancing an untenable general-
ization.

The latter part of the "Hymn of Beauty" provides a
link with the two following hymns of heavenly love and
beauty. In this latter part we are told that those who love
most truly able to form a spiritual ideal in their minds
which leads them away from frail earthly beauty to the
contemplation of heavenly beauty. In these last two hymns
Spenser gives up the classical mythology of the courtly
love tradition and speaks openly of the Christian conception of the love of God. There is not, of course, any fundamental opposition involved. Writers in the Renaissance
were very fond of using classical terms to express Christian ideas. When Spenser speaks of Cupid as existing before the world began and as making the world, he is merely
giving a classical form to Christian cosmology. When he

addresses Venus as the power of beauty leading to the propagation of the human race, he is at the same time thinking of God's creation of Adam and Eve in separate sexes and his command to increase and multiply. Therefore the essential difference between the two pairs of hymns is not that between pagan and Christian ideas but simply between earthly and heavenly love. Here on earth it is natural that we should give great weight to the personal aspects of love—our love for a member of the other sex, our love for a few close friends—but as we turn our thoughts to the great ideal of love, we must both intensify and expand our thoughts. We must expand them to a more generous love for our whole community, even for all mankind, and we must intensify them to contemplate the love of God.

The "Hymn of Heavenly Love" is an ecstatic praise of God's love for the world. Out of love he created the world, the angels, and man. Out of love for men seduced by the fallen angels he sent his Son to redeem them:

> O blessed well of love, O floure of grace,
> O glorious morning star, O lamp of light,
> Most lively image of thy Father's face,
> Eternall King of glory, Lord of might,
> Meeke lambe of God before all worlds behight,
> How can we thee requite for all this good?
> Or what can prize that thy most precious blood?

The reply is a poetical paraphrase of the command to love God with all our hearts, souls, and minds, and our neighbor as ourselves. The conclusion is a plea to give up all earthly loves for that mystical communion with God which repays the ascetic for the loss of all else:

> Then shall thy ravisht soule inspired bee
> With heavenly thoughts, farre above humane skill,
> And thy bright radiant eyes shall plainely see

[176]

The Poet of Love

> Th'Idee of his pure glorie, present still
> Before thy face, that all thy spirits shall fill
> With sweet enragement of celestiall love,
> Kindled through sight of those faire things above.

In the final hymn Spenser declares that through the beauty of the earth and the heavens we can get some idea of the unapproachable beauty of God. After describing the nine hierarchies of heaven he points out the figure of Sapience (Wisdom) sitting in the bosom of God and clad like a queen in royal robes. She becomes for Spenser the type and epitome of all beauty, the pure spiritual essence of that which we can only dimly appreciate on earth. She is the beloved of God. Whoever is permitted to behold her face shall have all joy, bliss, and happiness. This daring piece of symbolism, which seems to add a new person to the Trinity, is merely a very striking example of Spenser's habit of personifying abstract qualities. We have already noticed it in connection with Guyon and the palmer in the second book of the *Faerie Queene*. Here it is a convenient device to permit a description of the beauty of the deity. To have attempted to show us the beauty of God the Father, already described as unapproachable by human eyes, would have been to court certain failure. By inserting the figure of Sapience as a female figure, Spenser not only makes it possible to describe divine beauty but also creates an opportunity to declare its superiority to the beauty of Venus in the "Hymn of Love."

All these ideas are found in the *Faerie Queene* in a much less systematized way. The love of God, including a passage on the vision of the mystic, is the theme of Book I. In Book II we are shown the effects of pursuing mere bodily pleasure instead of true love, and in Book III that true love is personified in the figure of Britomart. Book

IV expands the scope of love to include friendship with individuals, while the theme of justice in Book V is its complete expansion to cover the whole community. In Book VI we are shown that the gentle heart, which alone can give rise to courtesy, is the result of generous unselfish love of others. The narrative group composed of Books III–V is especially devoted to problems of love. The number and variety of characters involved makes it possible for Spenser to introduce a great many different relations between lovers and to illustrate thoroughly what he approves and what he does not approve. In Britomart we have the woman in love searching for her lover, in Florimel the woman whose love is not reciprocated, in Amoret the woman who has been separated from her lover, in Belphoebe the cold beauty whose heart is not touched by the faithful devotion of a man. Psychological difficulties and even sex perversion are also included in this amazingly full and intricate pattern of case histories. The special virtue of Book III is that it holds up an ideal of a true, normal, and healthy love without being sanctimonious or prudish. Spenser can laugh with the squire of dames at his cynical tale of sexual adventures, and he takes a frankly sympathetic attitude toward Hellenore's enthusiastic affair with Paridell after some years of neglect at the hands of the impotent miser Malbecco, but his four heroines are all in their different ways inspiring and appealing examples of purity of heart.

Three passages in the *Faerie Queene* are especially connected with Spenser's conception of love: the Garden of Adonis in Book III, the Temple of Venus in Book IV, and the House of Holiness in Book I. It is interesting to note that the framework in the first case is that of classical mythology; in the second, medieval courtly love; and in the third, Christian doctrine. The Garden of Adonis has already been described in chapter vii in connection with the idea of mutability. What we are concerned with here is the Garden as a symbol of fertility. Nature here brings forth the seeds of all things according to their kinds:

> Infinite shapes of creatures there are bred,
> And uncouth formes, which none yet ever knew,
> And every sort is in a sundry bed
> Set by itselfe, and ranckt in comely rew:
> Some fit for reasonable soules t'indew,
> And some made for beasts, some made for birds to weare,
> And all the fruitful spawne of fishes hew
> In endless ranks along enranged were,
> That seem'd the ocean could not containe them there.

Wicked Time, who brings decay and death, is the enemy of this plenitude of creation, and so there must be constant reproduction of all the species. Here sweet love exists without rancor or jealousy:

> Franckly each paramour his leman knowes,
> Each bird his mate, ne any does envie
> Their goodly merriment, and gay felicitie.

In the midst of this paradise is the arbor of Venus and Adonis, who are the great symbols of fertility. Adonis is subject to mortality, but as the male principle he is "father of forms" and so is "eterne in mutabilitie," for the system of nature depends upon him. The thought seems to be that by the creative sexual act he constantly renews himself. The whole story of the Garden is praise of the fertility and plenitude of nature, including man. Love here finds its place as the mainspring of an order of things subject to time. Men and animals, birds and fish, must all be moved by love to reproduce themselves and carry out the divine plan for the world.

Edmund Spenser and the Faerie Queene

The Temple of Venus is connected with the Garden of Adonis through the fact that Amoret, who has been brought up in the Garden, is found by her lover Scudamour in the Temple. We here progress from the universal principle of fertility to the individual search for a mate. Consequently the theme is that of courtship, and for it Spenser takes the setting of courtly love. Under the rules of this system the man must show patience and bravery in overcoming difficulties. After defeating twenty knights outside the Temple, Scudamour has to pass the two porters, Doubt and Delay, and the door guard, Daunger (Haughtiness or Aloofness). In the grounds are bands of lovers and also of faithful friends. This is the book of friendship, and Spenser wished to emphasize that friendship is only another form of love. On the porch of the Temple is Concord uniting the hands of Love and Hate. There is no place for Adonis in this picture, so Venus is described as covered with a veil because she has both sexes in herself. She alone is the complete symbol of fertility here, begetting and conceiving without other aid. To her the assembled lovers sing a hymn praising her as creator and maintainer of the world and pacifier of all rage and conflict:

Great Venus, queene of beautie and of grace,
The joy of gods and men, that under skie
Doest fayrest shine and most adorne thy place,
That with thy smiling looke doest pacifie
The raging seas and makst the stormes to flie;
Thee, goddess, thee the winds, the clouds doe feare,
And when thou spredst thy mantle forth on hie;
The waters play and pleasant lands appeare,
And heavens laugh, and al the world shews joyous cheare.

. . . .

So all the world by thee at first was made,
And dayly yet thou doest the same repaire:

[180]

The Poet of Love

> Ne ought on earth that merry is and glad,
> Ne ought on earth that lovely is and fayre,
> But thou the same for pleasure didst prepayre.
> Thou art the root of all that joyous is,
> Great god of men and women, queene of th'ayre,
> Mother of laughter, and welspring of blisse,
> O graunt that of my love at last I may not misse.

It is significant that Venus is here addressed not just as the goddess of love in the narrow sense but as the creatrix of the world, the bringer of concord, and the source of everything that is lovely and fair. This is a great extension of the place of Venus in the Garden, where she appears only as the symbol of fertility. We have now a goddess who is the protectress of many of the finest things in life.

The House of Holiness is not linked by Spenser with his exposition of love in the later books. It is therefore all the more important to point out that it is very definitely a house of love as well as a house of holiness. Nor is this true only in the sense that the activities of the house are inspired by God's love for sinners. Divine love is indeed the spirit of the house, but the people in it also exemplify human love and the sexual relationship. One of the first things we learn about the inmates of the House of Holiness is that they are all in love—in the ordinary meaning of that phrase. Fidelia and Speranza are "spoused, yet wanting wedlock's solemnize," and Charissa is already linked in marriage. Her characteristic activity exemplifies fruitfulness:

> She was a woman in her freshest age,
> Of wondrous beauty, and of bountie rare,
> With goodly grace and comely personage,
> That was on earth not easie to compare;
> Full of great love, but Cupid's wanton snare
> As hell she hated, chaste in worke and will;

[181]

ind breasts were ever open bare,
reof her babes might sucke their fill;
s all in yellow robes arrayed still.

of babes about her hung,
sports, that joyd her to behold,
he fed, whiles they were weake and young,
put thrust them forth still as they wexed old:
And on her head she wore a tyre of gold,
Adorned with gemmes and owches wondrous faire,
Whose passing price uneath was to be told;
And by her side there sate a gentle paire
Of turtle doves, she sitting in an ivorie chaire.

Charissa, then, is the symbol of conjugal love and love of
posterity. It is she who takes the Red Cross Knight to
Mercy to be instructed in charitable acts toward the poor
and unfortunate, a connection which extends her love to
include all within its reach. As in the *Four Hymns* the
final state of love is the beatific vision of heavenly beauty;
so here, when the knight has received all he can at the
hands of Charissa and Mercy, he is led to the hermit Contemplation and given a sight of the New Jerusalem with
the blessed angels walking its streets "in gladsome com-
panee." But his request to be transported at once to the
joys of heaven is denied. Earthly love has its place in the
scheme of things as well as heavenly. We have our present
life to live, and in it love, on all its levels, plays the central
part. This seems to be Spenser's conclusion, no matter
where in his works we look; but we must remember that
his conception of love included and unified all those levels.
The physical desire to propagate, the spiritual union and
companionship of individuals, the divine love of God for
the world, these are all to Spenser part of one great cosmic
force. Like the Neo-Platonist, one is to rise from one level
to another, but in Spenser's thought the lower levels are

not denied by the upper ones and all have tremendous significance for man.

God's love toward man, a subject fully treated in the "Hymn of Heavenly Love," is also exemplified in the *Faerie Queene*. The examples come just where we would expect them in the first two books. Book I deals with the trials of a man attempting to combat sin. When at last this man is cast into the dungeon of Orgoglio, the splendid figure of Prince Arthur appears to rescue him. At the beginning of the eighth canto, in which the rescue occurs, are these significant lines:

> Ay me, how many perils do enfold
> The righteous man to make him daily fall,
> Were not that heavenly grace doth him uphold,
> And stedfast truth acquite him out of all?
> Her love is firme, her care continuall,
> So oft as he through his owne foolish pride
> Or weaknesse is to sinful bands made thrall:
> Else should this Redcrosse knight in bands have died,
> For whose deliverance she this prince doth thither guide.

Here we have two manifestations of God's love. Una, who is "stedfast truth" and in another sense is the church, continually expresses God's loving care for men. When the need is desperate, God sends special grace in the person of Arthur. As Spenser says, Una's care is continual. She intervenes with her own hand to save the knight from killing himself with Despair's knife, and it is she who takes him to the House of Holiness where the love of God is taught and practiced. In the eighth canto of Book II the hero is in a similarly desperate situation. Separated from all assistance, Guyon lies in a swoon on the ground. The palmer hears a voice calling him to the spot and finds a glorious angel keeping guard over Guyon. Spenser's comment on this forms an eloquent summary of his views on God's love for humanity:

And is there care in heaven? and is there love
In heavenly spirits to these creatures base,
That may compassion of their evils move?
There is: else much more wretched were the case
Of men than beasts. But O th'exceeding grace
Of highest God, that loves his creatures so,
And all his workes with mercy doth embrace,
That blessed angels he sends to and fro,
To serve to wicked man, to serve his wicked foe.

How oft do they their silver bowers leave,
To come to succor us, that succor want?
How oft do they with golden pineons cleave
The flitting skyes, like flying pursuivant,
Against foule feends to aid us millitant?
They for us fight, they watch and dewly ward,
And their bright squadrons round about us plant,
And all for love, and nothing for reward:
O why should heavenly God to men have such regard?

The Elizabethans believed unreservedly in the existence of the angels, a belief which contributed to many moving passages in their poetry. Here they are used as the proof of God's love for man, but the ultimate proof, as every Elizabethan knew, was that used by Spenser in the "Hymn of Heavenly Love"—the death of God's Son upon the cross. By this act God himself gave proof of the unity of love throughout the universe, the joining of divine and human love in a single dramatic act.

CONCLUSION

I HAVE tried to show that in Spenser's personality the man of action and the artist are inseparable. Had Spenser remained the bookish, high-brow poet of 1580, with his "Dreams" and "Courts of Cupid," we should never have had the great sweep of human action in the *Faerie Queene*. Now that we have seen him in his life and in his writings, what shall we say of Edmund Spenser? Obviously, like Raleigh, he was the Elizabethan man of action and empire-builder; equally obviously, like Shakespeare, whose travels led only to London, he was a master of words. Yet to one who has pondered long upon his character it is not those things that remain in the mind but two very human qualities—courage and loyalty. To his personal loves and hates he adhered with almost reckless tenacity. Fear of royal or noble disfavor never prevented him from advocating reforms or defending friends. Ordinary caution should have prevented him from openly attacking Burleigh, yet he did so with bitter satire. When Raleigh and Grey were in disgrace with Elizabeth, he defended them in the *Faerie Queene*. Cynics may remark that Spenser merely bet on the wrong horse and underrated the power of the opposition, but to do so is to miss an essential grain of obstinate honesty in Spenser's character which should be remembered when we sometimes look askance at the flattery so liberally sprinkled through his, as through other Elizabethan, works. Next, one sees in Spenser's rise from relative obscurity—not even the scientific methods of modern

[185]

research can discover who his parents were—a distinctly practical ability to deal with life and carve out a fortune. There is none of the supposed dreamy ineptitude once connected with poets to be seen in him. Although he failed in his ambition to advance at court—and the reasons for it are clear from what we have just said above—he seems to have improved every opportunity offered to him in Ireland in a business way. He died possessed of large estates sufficient to set up both his sons as landed gentlemen. And yet, like Shakespeare, this side of his character never obscured or overwhelmed the philosophic thinker and the idealistic poet. The two coexisted in a typically Elizabethan way. The Elizabethan gentleman could indulge in cutthroat rivalry and always had an eye for the main chance, but he was still under the spell of the Middle Ages. He knew the thirst of the soul, which as Ben Jonson said, doth ask a drink divine.

Spenser's mind could deal successfully with the difficulties of military and political life in Ireland, but it could also move serene and untroubled among the shepherds of Arcady and among the high gods in conclave on the top of Arlo Hill. And what these very gods were debating is ever the theme of Spenser's most characteristic thought, the theme of mutability. Why is life so unstable? Why is man called to tragedy and to heroism in this earthly life instead of to the placid enjoyment of the delights which the bounty of nature might provide us? Why must the Red Cross Knight, having seen the vision of the Heavenly City, return to the ugly and perilous business of fighting the dragon of this world's sins? The terminology has changed in the twentieth century but not the essential problem. Eliot and Auden are still debating why man, who has conquered nature and made the atoms do his will, sees himself surrounded with forces of evil which seem to nullify all his conquests. The Elizabethan tried to grasp both time and eternity. He failed but left behind him imperishable works of art as a record of his failure. The modern man, who has neglected things eternal and has seen things temporal consumed in the fires of destruction, seems likely not to do so well.

SUGGESTIONS FOR FURTHER READING

CHAPTER I

The best account of Elizabethan England is J. B. Black's *The Reign of Elizabeth* (Oxford, 1936). For a brief treatment of the Renaissance in general Wallace K. Ferguson's *The Renaissance* (New York, 1940) is excellent. The religious, social, and intellectual ideas of the time are ably discussed by Hardin Craig in *The Enchanted Glass* (New York, 1936) and by E. M. W. Tillyard in *The Elizabethan World Picture* (London, 1943).

CHAPTER II

Alexander C. Judson's excellent *Life of Edmund Spenser* (Baltimore, 1945) has made unnecessary the reading of other biographical material at present, unless one wishes to investigate the work of the scholars whose researches provided the materials for his synthesis. Of these, one might mention Mark Eccles, Douglas Hamer, Ray Heffner, Raymond Jenkins, and W. H. Welply (complete references in Judson's bibliography). One important article by Eccles, "Elizabethan Edmund Spensers," *Modern Language Quarterly*, V, 413–27, appeared after Judson's book was published.

CHAPTER III

The Johns Hopkins Variorum Edition of Spenser includes the *Shepherds' Calendar* in Volume I of the *Minor*

Poems (Baltimore, 1943) with excerpts from all the significant scholarship up to that time. There has been a hot debate on the identity of "E. K." Anyone interested in the question should look up and read the original articles by Kuersteiner, Jenkins, Starnes, and Mitchener. On the identification of characters with real people those readers who are impatient with my cautious attitude should read the important series of articles by Paul E. McLane, all of which have appeared since the publication of Volume I of the *Minor Poems*. These articles are found in the *Journal of English and Germanic Philology* (XLVI, 144–49, and XLIX, 324–32), *Modern Language Quarterly* (IX, 3–9), and *PMLA* (LXII, 936–49, and LXIV, 599). On Spenser's religious position I agree in general with Judson, with McLane, and with Virgil K. Whitaker in his recent *Religious Basis of Spenser's Thought* (Stanford, 1950). For the older opinion that Spenser was a Calvinistic Puritan see the books and articles by Padelford, Buyssens, and others excerpted in the Variorum Edition. Two more recent articles are those by J. B. Fletcher in *PMLA*, LVIII, 634–48, and by P. N. Siegel in *Studies in Philology*, XLI, 201–22.

CHAPTER IV

On the origin, nature, and development of Books III–V see Josephine W. Bennett, *The Evolution of the Faerie Queene* (Chicago, 1942). The work of other scholars on the separate problems can be followed in the volumes of the Variorum Edition. An excellent recent article on the problem of historical allegory is Allan H. Gilbert's essay on "Belphoebe's Misdeeming of Timias" in *PMLA*, LXII, 622–43.

Suggestions for Further Reading

CHAPTER V

A great deal of writing has been done on the moral and historical allegory of Books I and II. The best guides through this morass are the Variorum Edition and the discussion and references in Mrs. Bennett's book just referred to. An important recent article on some of the troublesome points in Book II is A. S. P. Woodhouse's "Nature and Grace in the *Faerie Queene*," in *ELH*, XVI, 194–228. Another valuable study, too late to be noticed by Mrs. Bennett or the Variorum editors, is M. Y. Hughes's article in the *Journal of the History of Ideas* (IV, 381–99), "Spenser's Acrasia and the Circe of the Renaissance."

CHAPTER VI

Almost all the important work on Book VI has been excerpted in the Variorum Edition. I can only add two articles: R. H. Pearce, "Primitivistic Ideas in the *Faerie Queene*," *Journal of English and Germanic Philology*, XLIV, 139–51, and J. C. Maxwell, "The Truancy of Calidore," *ELH*, XIX, 143–49.

CHAPTER VII

The debate over the sources and philosophic implications of the Mutability Cantos will be found excerpted in the Variorum Edition. Since that time three articles have appeared: H. A. Kahin, "Spenser and the School of Alanus," *ELH*, VIII, 257–72; Milton Miller, "Nature in the *Faerie Queene*," *ELH*, XVIII, 191–200; and M. K. Woodworth, "The Mutability Cantos and the Succession," *PMLA*, LIX, 985–1002.

CHAPTER VIII

Spenser's treatment of love as a whole has been discussed only by C. S. Lewis in the *Allegory of Love* and by Janet Spens in *Spenser's Faerie Queene*. Both chapters are excellent. Special aspects of the theme have been discussed in connection with the Garden of Adonis and the Court of Venus. See the writers excerpted in the Variorum Edition for Books III and IV.

INDEX